THE ART OF
PROMPT ENGINEERING

FROM CONFUSED TO CONFIDENT: THE SKILL
THAT MAKES AI WORK FOR YOU

_____

Ayan Khan

AYAN KHAN

THE ART OF PROMPT ENGINEERING
Copyright © 2025 by Ayan Khan

Printed by Amazon Kindle Direct Publishing (KDP)

Cover design by Ayan Khan
Published independently by Ayan Khan

DEDICATION

To Ayan Khan

For not giving up when the path felt uncertain.

For embracing the unknown with curiosity and courage.

This book is a reminder that passion, when shared with purpose, becomes power.

Here's to the journey, the growth, and the fire that never fades.

Table of Contents

AUTHOR'S NOTE

This book is the result of a deep passion for asking the right questions, diving into the power of language, and guiding others to tap into the limitless possibilities of prompts.

It's not just a guide; it's a journey that's been mine, one filled with struggles, breakthroughs, and moments that changed my perspective in ways I never imagined.

My hope is that as you read, you'll feel inspired to ask bold, meaningful questions, to challenge the way you think, and to find the courage to explore what truly matters in your own life.

~ Ayan Khan

DISCLAIMER

This book is intended for educational and inspirational purposes only. While every effort has been made to ensure the accuracy and usefulness of the content, the author makes no guarantees and assumes no responsibility for how this information is used.

Some sections have been developed and refined with the assistance of artificial intelligence tools to improve clarity, flow, and engagement. Readers are encouraged to verify critical information independently, especially when making important decisions.

This book is a reflection of personal experiences, knowledge, and exploration. Please read with an open mind and a spirit of curiosity.

Thank you for being part of this journey.

PREFACE

This book comes from a deep, personal curiosity, a curiosity about language, the art of asking the right questions, and the way they can change everything. What started as a quiet exploration in my own mind soon became something I felt compelled to share. It hasn't been a perfect journey. There were struggles, doubts, and plenty of moments when I wasn't sure I could make sense of it all. But there were also breakthroughs, small, unexpected moments that made everything worthwhile. Through it, I've learned more than I expected, not only about prompts but about the way we learn, grow, and navigate the world with the questions we ask.

Writing this book wasn't just about putting together information. It was about sharing something real, my journey, my growth, and the insights I've gathered along the way. My hope is that, as you read these pages, you feel something stir inside you that you'll walk away not only with new knowledge but with the courage to ask deeper, bolder questions. Maybe even challenge the things you thought you knew.

If you ever have questions, if something resonates with you or sparks more curiosity, I'm here. I want to help, to be part of your journey. Feel free to reach out to me during business hours [Mon-Fri, 10:30 am – 5:00 pm IST].

Email: ayaankhann@gmail.com

Thank you for joining me in this adventure. I'm truly grateful that you're here.

INTRODUCTION

Welcome to the World of Prompt Engineering

Ever stared at a blinking cursor, trying to figure out how to get something smart out of an AI and felt like you were negotiating with a super-polite alien who's read everything but still needs directions? Yeah, you're exactly where you need to be.

This isn't just a book. It's a kind of road trip through one of the most exciting and weirdly human parts of artificial intelligence: prompt engineering. And don't worry, you don't need a PhD or a background in machine learning to come along. Whether you're a curious beginner, a tech-savvy tinkerer, or someone who just wants to use AI to work smarter, not harder, there's something here for you.

But before we start pulling apart prompts and hacking together beautifully efficient inputs, let's take a moment to answer a simple (but surprisingly slippery) question.

What Is Prompt Engineering?

Imagine trying to ask a genie for a wish, but the genie is a language model, and it takes everything you say very literally. Welcome to prompt engineering.

At its core, prompt engineering is the art and, yes, it really is an art, of crafting the right input to get the output you want from an AI system. It's part communication, part experimentation, and part wizardry. You're essentially learning how to speak fluently with machines that "understand" only in patterns, probabilities, and predictions.

Let's break it down a bit:

- **Crafting Instructions:** Think of prompts like recipes. The clearer and more specific your ingredients (instructions), the better your final dish (response). It's less like coding and more like composing a very clever email to a robot who's read the entire internet but still needs direction.

- **Leveraging AI's Weird Superpowers:** These models can summarize books, debug code, draft marketing copy, or write a love letter to your houseplants. But they won't do any of it well unless you ask the right way. Prompt engineering unlocks those superpowers.

- **A Moving Target:** Unlike traditional software, language models are fuzzy on the edges. A tiny tweak, a word swapped here, a phrase restructured there, can produce

radically different responses. This makes it powerful, but also... kind of frustrating.

- **Trial and Error Is the Game:** Your first prompt won't be perfect. That's okay. In fact, it's expected. Prompt engineering is iterative, like sculpting out of clay, not carving marble. You mold, test, adjust, repeat.

Why Prompt Engineering Matters

Let's get something out of the way: AI isn't magic. But knowing how to talk to it? That's pretty close.

- **It's Not What You Ask, It's How You Ask:** Even the most advanced models can sound confused or go completely off track if you give them vague or poorly structured prompts. Prompt engineering is how you turn generic AI into a smart, creative collaborator.

- **Creativity + Productivity Boost:** Want to brainstorm business ideas? Summarize a dense article? Generate song lyrics about pickles in the style of Taylor Swift? The right prompt can help you do all of that, better and faster.

11

- **No PhD Needed:** That's the beauty. You don't need to understand neural networks or gradient descent. If you can ask good questions and think critically, you can harness AI. Prompt engineering democratizes access to sophisticated tools.

- **Fuel for Innovation:** From startups building GPT-powered apps to students writing smarter essays, prompt engineering is opening doors. It's not just about outputs, it's about asking better questions, exploring new ideas, and solving old problems in new ways.

- **Ethics Are Not Optional:** AI mirrors the data it was trained on, and that mirror is often cracked. Prompt engineers must be aware of biases, limitations, and unintended consequences. It's not just about using the tool, but using it wisely.

How AI Works – For Newcomers

Let's lift the hood, just a bit. Don't worry, we'll keep it Easy.

- **Data + Algorithms = Magic:** AI models like GPT/Claude/Gemini/Grox are trained on billions of words, books, articles, websites, you name it. They learn to recognize patterns, not meaning. Think of it like a statistical autocomplete on steroids.

- **Language Models:** These systems guess the next word based on what you've written so far. They don't "understand" you in the way people do, but they're ridiculously good at sounding like they do.

- **Neural Networks – The Brains Behind the Bot:** At the core of these models are neural networks, systems designed to mimic how the human brain works. They're made up of layers of connected nodes, kind of like digital neurons, that take in information and learn from it over time. Thanks to their complexity, these networks can take on advanced tasks like translating languages, summarizing text, and even generating creative writing.

- **Prompts Are the Remote Control:** You tell the AI what to do through a prompt. The more context and clarity you give, the better it performs. It's not cheating, it's skill.

- **It's All About Iteration:** Remember, AI doesn't "know" anything in the way we do. It guesses. So writing prompts becomes an ongoing dance of testing, tweaking, and refining.

What's New

In a field that's moving this fast, keeping up with the latest ideas and breakthroughs is essential. This book captures the newest trends and advancements in prompt engineering. Here's what's fresh and exciting in this edition:

- **Next-Level Prompting Techniques:** You'll learn about layered prompts, chain-of-thought reasoning, multi-modal magic (yes, image + text!), and more. This is stuff most people haven't even heard of, yet.

- **Real-World Examples:** From marketing to writing novels, you'll see how prompt engineering plays out in the wild. We've packed this book with case studies, so theory never floats far from practice.

- **A Bigger Focus on Ethics:** Bias, misinformation, prompt injection attacks, we're covering the shadows too. AI isn't neutral, and prompt engineering comes with responsibility. (We'll help you carry it.)

- **Interactive Tools & Exercises:** Checklists. Troubleshooting tips. Prompts to try. This book is as much a sandbox as it is a manual.

- **Voices from the Field:** You'll hear from industry experts, prompt nerds, and AI experimenters who are in the thick of it. Their stories, tips, and facepalm-worthy mistakes will help you level up faster.

How to Use This Book

This book is designed to take you step by step, from the fundamentals all the way to advanced prompt engineering techniques. To help you get the most out of it, here are a few tips:

- **Modular Format:** Feel free to skip around. Each module builds on the last, but if you're itching to dive into advanced strategies or ethical quandaries, jump ahead. You won't break anything.

- **Hands-On Learning:** Try the exercises. Tweak the examples. Break stuff. Learn by doing, not just reading.

- **Checklists = Your New Best Friends:** At the end of each chapter, you'll find quick summaries and tips. Use them like sticky notes for your brain.

- **Make Mistakes:** Seriously. Prompt engineering is about experimentation. Let your curiosity lead, and don't be afraid of a few AI hiccups along the way.

- **Think Critically:** Just because a model gives you a slick-sounding answer doesn't mean it's correct, or ethical. Pause. Reflect. Revise. That's the prompt engineer's code.

- **Keep Evolving:** This field moves fast. AI today isn't the same as AI six months from now. Stay curious. Keep testing. Join communities. You're now part of a movement.

Ready?

Let's unlock the magic behind the machine, one prompt at a time.

Prompting Exercises:

Now it's your turn to put what you've learned into action. Try the exercises below to deepen your understanding and sharpen your prompting skills.

This book is not intended to remain untouched on a shelf or forgotten in a downloads folder. It is designed to be actively engaged with, annotated, tested, and explored through hands-on use. The more you interact with it, the more value you'll gain. Prompt engineering isn't something you just learn, it's something you do.

Each chapter includes hands-on experiments, challenges, and practice labs that turn theory into working muscle memory. Whether you're a curious beginner or already experimenting with advanced techniques, these exercises will help you sharpen your skills and develop real intuition.

Here's how to get started:

Prompt Lab 1: Play with the Ocean

After reading **"What Is Prompt Engineering?"**, let's get our feet wet, literally.

Goal: Understand how even small changes in a prompt can dramatically shift an AI's tone, style, and response.

Try This:

- Open any AI tool you like (ChatGPT, Claude, etc.).

- Type:

  "Write a paragraph about the ocean."

- Now remix the prompt:

  - "Write a poetic paragraph about the ocean."

  - "Give me a scientific explanation of ocean currents."

  - "Describe the ocean as if you're a pirate."

Look For:

- How does the language, detail, and voice change?

- Which prompt gives you the most compelling or useful response?

- What happens when you're vague vs. laser-specific?

Why It Matters: This is prompt engineering in action. A few extra words can take you from a Wikipedia entry to a scene straight out of Pirates of the Caribbean.

Mini Project: Your Prompt Playground

After **"How AI Works: A Beginner's Overview"**, it's time to build your sandbox.

Goal: Create a personal "Prompt Journal" where you can test ideas, document your results, and track your growth.

What You'll Need:

- A doc, a Notion page, or even a paper notebook.

- Set up columns like

  Prompt | Purpose | Output Summary | What Worked | What Didn't

Example Entry:

- **Prompt:** "Summarize this article in 3 bullet points."

- **Purpose:** Content summarization

- **Output:** Good overall but missed one key point

- **What Worked:** Bullet format applied.

- **What Didn't:** Needed clearer context

How It Helps: This becomes your prompt database, like a recipe book for future you.

Rework the Basics: Prompt Makeover Challenge

After **"Why Prompt Engineering Matters"**, take these common tasks and upgrade the prompts.

Task	Default Prompt	Improved Prompt
Write an email	"Write an email."	"Write a polite, professional email requesting a meeting to review a new campaign idea."
Fix some code	"Fix this code."	"Explain what's wrong with this Python snippet and show a corrected version with comments."
Get blog ideas	"Give me blog ideas."	"Suggest 10 catchy blog titles about eco-friendly travel for an audience of Gen Z travelers."

What to Do: Try both versions. Compare the results. What was missing from the default prompt? What did the improved version do better?

Creative Prompting Sprint: Just for Fun

This one's optional, but highly recommended if you're feeling curious.

Challenge: Write prompts that make the AI do these things:

1. Write a Riddle.

2. Explain quantum physics to a 10-year-old

3. Create a riddle that ends with a pun

4. Plan a 5-day digital detox retreat

Bonus Level: Tweak each prompt to see how you can make the response more creative, more accurate, or more "you."

Final Tip: Reflect, Revisit, Revise

Every few chapters, go back to your earlier prompts and rework them with your new skills. You'll be amazed at how quickly your intuition improves.

CHAPTER 1

UNDERSTANDING PROMPTS

Before we can talk about engineering anything, let's just slow down and look at the humble prompt. That one little line you type in, the one that kicks off the whole conversation with an AI. It might seem simple (and sometimes it is), but under the surface? It's doing a lot more than you think.

This chapter is where we lay the groundwork. We're going to unpack what a prompt actually is, why it matters more than you probably realize, and how something as tiny as a word choice can tilt an entire AI response in one direction or another. If you want to shape what the AI gives you back, it starts here, with how you ask.

Whether you're here to write smarter content, get clearer answers, or just mess around creatively with a machine that knows a lot but still needs a little guidance, this chapter is your starting line.

What Is a Prompt?

Let's not overcomplicate it. A **prompt** is just something you tell an AI to get it to respond. That's it. It's your message, your input, your ask. Think of it like tossing the first pitch in a game, the ball's in your hand, and the AI's just waiting to react.

It might be something small like:

"What's the weather in Tokyo?"

Or something layered and kind of theatrical like:

"Act like a career coach and help me prepare for a job interview in the tech industry."

Same basic idea you're giving the AI a setup. What you say determines what it throws back at you and here's the thing nobody tells you: **how you ask is often more important than what you ask.** That one sentence, your prompt, is your steering wheel. Turn it the right way, and suddenly you're driving toward way better results.

What Makes a Prompt... Work?

There's no magic formula, but there are a few qualities that show up over and over in good prompts. Let's break them down:

- **Clarity** – Say what you mean. Skip the fluff. Be plain if you need to be.

- **Context** – Give the AI a bit of the story. Otherwise, it's like asking someone to finish your sentence without knowing what you were talking about.

- **Purpose** – What are you actually hoping to get back? Be honest about your goal, it'll help you phrase things better.

- **Specificity** – Vague inputs get vague results. If you want sharp, smart answers, aim your questions with precision.

You don't need all four every time, but the more you hit, the better your results usually get.

Why Prompts Matter (More Than You Think)

A lot of people treat prompts like search terms. But with AI, you're not querying a database, you're **collaborating** with a machine that can generate, not just retrieve. And that changes the game.

Here's what a good prompt can do:

- **Guide the output** – You're telling the AI what kind of answer you want.

- **Shape tone and structure** – Need something academic? Casual? Weirdly poetic? You're the director.

- **Handle complexity** – Good prompts can chain tasks, walk the AI through multi-step processes, or simulate scenarios. Think of it like teaching a class: don't just give the topic, explain the assignment.

Prompts are how you talk to the AI, but also how you teach it to talk back the way you need.

Quick Flashback: Prompts, Then and Now

Back in the day, "prompts" were cold, coded instructions, if you weren't a developer, good luck. But now? You can talk to an AI almost like you'd talk to a person. You don't need to know syntax. You just need to know how to communicate clearly, like… a curious, slightly bossy human.

This shift, from rigid commands to fluid, natural prompts, has made AI feel less like a tool and more like a creative partner. (Weird, right?)

Why Prompt Engineering Is a Big Deal

Let's get real. Prompting well is like learning to ask better questions in life. It gives you an edge. Here's what that edge gets you:

- **Faster, better results** – Less time spent fixing clunky answers.

- **No coding required** – Just language. The stuff you already use every day.

- **Unlocks creativity** – Want to write a story? Analyze market trends? Simulate a courtroom cross-examination? The prompt is your remote control.

Once you get the hang of it, the whole process gets faster and more intuitive, like tuning a radio and suddenly hitting the sweet spot.

Anatomy of an Effective Prompt

The best prompts usually include some combo of the following:

- **Clear instructions** – Not "Tell me about space," but "Summarize three current challenges with space tourism."

- **Relevant context** – If it matters to the task, mention it. "Assume the reader is a 12-year-old." That sort of thing.

- **Requested output format** – Want bullet points? A limerick? A LinkedIn post? Say so.

- **Openness to refinement** – Try, revise, repeat. Your first draft doesn't have to be perfect. It's a process.

Common Challenges in Prompt Design

Even seasoned prompt folks mess this up sometimes. Here's where it usually goes sideways:

- **Too vague** – "Talk about climate change" will give you a Wikipedia-lite dump. Be sharper.

- **Overstuffed** – Don't cram eight tasks into one prompt. Break it up.

- **Context collapse** – If it's a long thread, the AI might forget earlier bits. Remind it.

- **Bias sneak-in** – Your phrasing might nudge the AI in weird directions. Be aware. Be intentional.

Prompt Tweaks in Action

Watch how changing just one thing shifts the whole vibe:

1. **Plain**

   o Prompt: "Explain renewable energy."

   o Result: A textbook-style overview.

2. **With Focus**

   o Prompt: "Explain renewable energy, especially solar power in urban areas."

   o Result: More targeted, location-aware insights.

3. **With Tone**

   o Prompt: "Explain renewable energy in a fun, kid-friendly way."

- o Result: Think metaphors, jokes, and simpler language.

Small change → big ripple.

Prompt Lab: Practice Box

Let's make it real. Don't just read, play. Test. Rewrite.

Exercise 1: Remix a Prompt

Pick your favorite book and try this:

- **A.** "Summarize this book."

- **B.** "Summarize it like a snarky movie critic."

- **C.** "Summarize it in three bullet points."

Notice what changes in tone, detail, and delivery.

Exercise 2: Add Some Context

Try asking:

- "Make a travel itinerary."

- Then ask:

- "Make a 3-day Paris itinerary with museums, local cafés, and hidden gems."

Which one makes you want to pack a bag?

Exercise 3: Fix a Flop

Dig up an old prompt you used that got a boring response. Rewrite it with more detail and direction.

Example:

- Before: "Tell me about technology."

- After: "Explain how smartphones have changed remote work, especially in creative industries."

Then run both and compare. See what you learn.

Mini Project: Start a Prompt Journal

Make this a habit. Start a document or notebook where you:

- Record your prompts

- Note what you were trying to get

- Analyze what worked (and didn't)

- Add tweaks or future ideas

This becomes your custom prompt lab. It'll help you track progress and build muscle memory faster than you think.

Quick Recap

In this chapter, you've learned:

- **What prompts are** and why they matter.

- **How prompts shape AI behavior**, tone, and accuracy.

- **What makes prompts effective**, from clarity to context?

- **Common mistakes** to watch out for.

- **Real-world examples** that show prompt variation in action.

If this chapter left you with one takeaway, let it be this: you're not just asking the AI for stuff, you're teaching it how to talk to you.

Next up: **Crafting Basic Prompts.** We'll go deeper into structure, sequences, and how to make your requests more purpose-driven and powerful. Bring your prompt journal. It's about to earn its keep.

CHAPTER 2
CRAFTING BASIC PROMPTS

Or, How to Stop Talking Vaguely to Robots and Actually Get What You Want

There's something deceptively magical about typing a few words into a box and watching a model generate an answer out of the digital ether. But here's the thing, like any relationship, good communication is everything. AI models are smart, but not psychic. They thrive on specificity. If you don't know what you're asking, they won't know how to answer (and trust me, they will guess, usually wrong, sometimes hilariously so).

This chapter is your toolkit for crafting basic prompts that work, like, really work. Whether you're just starting out or already tinkering with more advanced stuff, learning to write better prompts is like learning to ask better questions. The kind that unlock doors instead of rattling them. We'll break down the principles, show you exactly how they work in the wild, and yeah, there's a practice lab at the end.

Principles of Crafting Basic Prompts

Let's start with the fundamentals. Building a prompt is a bit like giving someone directions, only instead of telling them how to get to your favorite taco truck, you're guiding a language model through a conceptual forest, trying not to let it wander off into the philosophical weeds.

1. Clarity

This is your compass. Without it, everything goes sideways.

- **Be Concise:** Say what you mean without dragging it out. Think elevator pitch, not three-part miniseries.

- **Avoid Ambiguity:** The AI can interpret "Tell me about history" in roughly a million ways. Don't make it guess.

Bad Prompt: "Tell me about history."

Better Prompt: "Provide a brief overview of the American Revolutionary War, including key causes and outcomes."

Why it works: It gives the model a time period, a focus, and a format. No guessing = better results.

2. Specificity

If clarity is the compass, specificity is the map.

- **Detail Matters:** The more grounded the request, the more grounded the answer.

- **Define the Scope:** What exactly do you want to cover? A topic? A timeframe? A specific audience?

Broad: "Explain renewable energy."

Specific: "Explain how solar energy contributes to sustainable development in urban areas."

This version avoids "renewable energy" as a whole textbook and zooms in on one slice. It's focused, manageable, and informative.

3. Context

Without context, the AI fills in blanks. Sometimes helpfully. Sometimes with unicorns and conspiracy theories.

- **Provide Background:** Tell it what it needs to know, just like you would when onboarding a new teammate.

- **Set Expectations:** Want a list? A paragraph? A rap in iambic pentameter? Say so.

Prompt: "List five key benefits of regular exercise for cardiovascular health in bullet-point format."

This prompt does all the things: it gives a topic, a format, a purpose, and even hints at tone (informative, health-related).

4. Purpose

This one's sneaky. A prompt might be clear, specific, and contextual, but if it doesn't know why you're asking, it can still go off-script.

- **Define the Goal:** Is this for teaching? Writing? Brainstorming? Fun? Serious analysis?

- **Target Outcome:** Want a story? A bulleted breakdown? A heartfelt essay? Say so.

Example 1 (Informative): "Describe the impact of renewable energy on local economies in a brief paragraph."

Example 2 (Creative): "Generate a short story about a future city powered entirely by wind energy."

Same topic, totally different goals. The difference is in the prompt's soul.

Strategies for Effective Basic Prompts

Knowing the rules is one thing. Using them skillfully is where the real fun starts. Like baking bread, sure, you can follow the recipe, but once you start improvising with spices, that's when it gets interesting.

Start with a Draft

Write a prompt like you're explaining your idea to a slightly confused but well-meaning friend. Then re-read it. Did you actually ask what you meant to?

"What exactly am I asking for? Could this be misunderstood? Did I just say 'write a poem about trees' when I meant 'make me cry about autumn leaves'?"

Iterative Refinement

- **Test It:** Run it. See what you get.

- **Tweak It:** Add a detail. Change the tone. Switch formats. You'll be shocked how much power lives in one extra word.

This is prompt engineering's version of debugging: same logic, less code, more existential AI vibes.

Use Examples and Templates

When you find a structure that works, keep it. Templates are your secret weapon.

Example Template:

"Summarize the following [TEXT] in [NUMBER] bullet points, focusing on [TOPIC/ASPECT]."

It's flexible. Reusable. Like a well-loved hoodie for your prompts.

Feedback Loop

Keep a **prompt journal**. No, seriously. Write down the good ones. Also the bad ones. Especially the weird ones that gave unexpectedly genius answers. Over time, you'll start to see patterns. And once you notice what works consistently, you're no longer guessing. You're iterating.

Practical Examples of Basic Prompts

Let's go from theory to street-level examples. Here's how principles and strategies play out in real prompts.

Example 1: Informative Request

Prompt:

"Describe the main causes of climate change, focusing on human activities. Provide your answer in a concise paragraph."

Why it works:

- Clear focus on "human activities."

- Specific format: "concise paragraph."

It tells the model what to say and how to say it. You'll get an answer you can use, not just skim and sigh.

Example 2: Creative Task

Prompt:

"Write a short poem about autumn in a small town, emphasizing the colorful changes in nature and a sense of nostalgia."

Why it works:

- Creative tone with emotional direction ("nostalgia").

- Strong visual cues ("colorful changes in nature").

It's like giving the model a watercolor palette and asking it to paint you a memory.

Example 3: Directive for Structure

Prompt:

"List three key strategies for improving productivity in an office setting, and explain each in two sentences."

Why it works:

- Structure = built in.

- Clarity = baked into the format.

- Scope = narrowed ("office setting," "three strategies").

Challenges and Common Pitfalls

Even with good intentions, it's easy to stumble. Here are the common banana peels:

Overly Broad Prompts

- **Problem:** You get a vague or generic answer.

- **Fix:** Add a time, place, or detail.

Instead of: "Explain economics."

Try: "Summarize the core principles of Keynesian economics as they apply to post-recession recovery efforts."

Ambiguity in Language

- **Problem:** The model misreads your tone or goal.

- **Fix:** Be literal. This is not the time for subtle metaphors (unless you want a metaphorical answer).

Inadequate Context

- **Problem:** You get filler or fluff.

- **Fix:** Feed the model what it needs, background, tone, target format. Don't let it guess.

Prompt Lab: Practice Box

Exercise 1: Rewrite and Refine

- **Task:** Take a broad, vague prompt and give it a clarity makeover.

  - **Original:** "Explain technology."

  - **Refined:** "Describe how smartphones have transformed communication over the past decade, with an emphasis on social media's role."

Exercise 2: Structure Challenge

- **Task:** Build a prompt that includes both structure and limits.

  - **Example:** "List five steps to organize a successful webinar, and explain each in one sentence."

- **Goal:** See how the AI snaps to attention with firm instructions.

Exercise 3: Explore Variations

- **Task:** Write two versions of the same idea, one vague, one detailed.

    o **Vague:** "Talk about healthy eating."

    o **Detailed:** "Explain three key benefits of a balanced diet that includes vegetables, fruits, and lean proteins. Use bullet points."

- **Compare:** Watch how much clearer, more useful the second response is.

Quick Recap

Here's what we covered (but not like, boringly summarized, think of this as your final power-up):

- Be **clear**. Seriously. Cut the fluff.

- Be **specific**. Precision beats poetry (most of the time).

- Provide **context**. Don't make the AI guess.

- Know your **purpose**. Ask yourself: "Why am I asking this?"

By now, you've got the basics under your belt. You can spot a vague prompt from a mile away and reshape it into something sharp and effective. Keep experimenting. Keep refining. And don't be afraid to talk to the AI like it's a very eager intern who's brilliant but easily distracted.

In the next chapter, we're going to play with prompt variations. Minor changes. Big shifts in results. It's where things get weird, and way more powerful. Keep that Prompt Lab open. You're going to need it.

CHAPTER 3

EXPLORING VARIATIONS

So, you've got the basics down, your prompts are clear, specific, purposeful, and contextual. Great! Now it's time to flex those creative muscles and dive into the slightly more experimental (and honestly, really fun) side of prompt engineering: **variations**.

In this chapter, we'll explore how even tiny tweaks to a prompt, switching a word, changing the tone, adding context, can completely reshape the AI's response. Think of it like seasoning a dish: a little more salt, a touch of spice, and suddenly the whole flavor changes. The same happens with prompts.

We'll cover why prompt variations matter, how to intentionally explore them, and what strategies you can use to discover what works best. You'll get hands-on with examples and exercises that sharpen your instincts and help you build your very own toolbox of variations.

The Rationale Behind Prompt Variations

Here's the thing: AI models are incredibly sensitive to language. The way you phrase something? It matters, a lot. Exploring prompt variations helps you:

- **Find the sweet spot in phrasing.** Some words unlock deeper, smarter responses. Others might lead you straight into generic territory.

- **Set the right tone.** Whether you're aiming for academic rigor, a casual chat, or a playful poem, phrasing shapes voice.

- **Understand AI behavior.** Tweaking prompts helps you see how the model "thinks," letting you anticipate quirks and finesse your requests.

- **Build prompt resilience.** Having multiple ways to ask for the same thing ensures flexibility, if one version flops, another might sing.

In short, variation is both your tuning fork and your parachute.

Strategies for Exploring Prompt Variations

Let's break down how you can systematically explore variations without going in circles.

A. Make Incremental Changes

Start small. Keep a base prompt and shift just one thing, maybe swap out a verb, add a clarifier, or change the structure slightly.

Example:

- **Base:** "Explain the benefits of exercise."

- **Tweak 1:** "List three major benefits of daily exercise for mental health."

- **Tweak 2:** "Describe how regular exercise improves physical and emotional well-being."

Each change narrows the scope or shifts the framing, which affects the output. Run these back-to-back and compare.

B. Flip the Structure

Changing the **format** of your prompt can have dramatic effects on how the AI structures its answer.

Example:

- **Narrative:** "Tell a story about how exercise improved someone's life."

- **List:** "List three ways exercise enhances quality of life."

- **Hybrid:** "Provide three bullet points on the benefits of exercise, with one explanatory sentence per point."

Different formats = different styles of thinking for the AI.

C. Play with Context and Detail

Sometimes vague prompts unleash creativity. Other times they return... fluff. Dialing the level of detail up or down helps you strike the right balance for your goal.

Example:

- **Basic:** "Discuss the impact of technology."

- **Focused:** "Discuss how social media affects teen communication habits."

- **Detailed:** "Explain how Instagram and TikTok influence teen self-esteem and social interaction, using recent trends as examples."

You're not just asking better questions, you're giving the model a richer stage to perform on.

D. Adjust Tone and Perspective

One of the most powerful levers you can pull: **how** the response should sound. Play with tone (funny vs. serious) and speaker perspective (expert vs. newbie).

Example:

- **Humorous:** "Explain gravity like you're doing stand-up comedy."

- **Formal:** "Provide an academic summary of gravitational theory for a physics journal."

- **Roleplay:** "As Isaac Newton, explain how you discovered gravity after your infamous apple moment."

This isn't just fun, it trains you to think like a tone-tuner, not just a prompt crafter.

Detailed Examples of Prompt Variations

Time to see all this in action. Here are three sets of prompts that show how small shifts = big results.

Example 1: Summarizing Content

- **Original:** "Summarize the article about climate change."

- **Variation A:** "Give a two-sentence summary of the climate change article."

- **Variation B:** "List the main causes, current impacts, and possible solutions to climate change from the article in bullet points."

Takeaway: The first is fast and broad. The second is concise. The third is structured and task-specific.

Example 2: Creative Writing

- **Original:** "Write a story about adventure."

- **Variation A:** "Write a vivid short story about an epic adventure in a mysterious jungle."

- **Variation B:** "From the perspective of a young explorer, write a story about navigating a mystical jungle filled with magical creatures."

Takeaway: A single added element, like perspective, can deepen character, plot, and tone.

Example 3: Technical Explanation

- **Original:** "Explain blockchain."

- **Variation A:** "Explain blockchain like you're teaching a 10-year-old."

- **Variation B:** "Break down how blockchain works, including key components like hashing, consensus mechanisms, and decentralization."

Takeaway: The first makes the concept approachable. The second leans into detail and audience expertise.

Common Pitfalls When Exploring Variations

Variation is powerful, but not without its traps. Here's how to avoid the big ones:

Changing Too Much at Once

If you tweak three things and get a better result, which change helped? Who knows?

- **Fix:** Change one variable at a time. Think of it like A/B testing.

Overloading the Prompt

Adding every possible detail can backfire, over-explaining might confuse the model or produce bloated responses.

- **Fix:** Keep prompts crisp. Layer in complexity gradually.

Ignoring the Audience

Prompts that work great for developers might not hit the mark with educators or creatives.

- **Fix:** Always keep your audience in mind. Who are you writing for? Match the tone and format accordingly.

Prompt Lab: Practice Box

Let's put this into action.

Exercise 1: Incremental Tweaks

- **Task:** Start with: "Explain the benefits of meditation."

  1. Basic version.

  2. Add structure: "List three benefits with one sentence each."

  3. Add tone: "Do it in a calming, reflective voice."

- **Goal:** Observe how tone and structure shift the feel and clarity of the response.

Exercise 2: Structure Experiment

- **Task:** Pick a historical event. Write one prompt for a narrative, one for a bullet-point summary.

- **Goal:** Compare which format helps you better understand or use the information.

Mini Project: Variation Portfolio

- **Steps:**

  1. Choose a theme (e.g., climate, AI, education).

  2. Create five different prompt styles: summary, story, formal, casual, bullet list.

  3. Record the outputs.

  4. Analyze what worked and why.

- **Outcome:** Your very own prompt variation toolkit for future use.

Quick Recap

Let's recap what we explored in this chapter:

- **Why variations matter:** They reveal tone, structure, and phrasing patterns that get better results.

- **How to explore them:** Tweak incrementally, experiment with format, play with tone and context.

- **What to watch for:** Don't change too much at once, avoid overcomplication, and always remember your audience.

- **How to grow:** Use exercises and a variation portfolio to continually sharpen your instincts.

Prompt variation isn't just about getting more creative, it's about getting more precise, more adaptive, and more insightful. It's where prompt engineering stops feeling mechanical and starts feeling like an art form.

In the next chapter, we'll shift gears and dive into **Building Contextual Prompts**, the art of shaping conversations that truly get the moment. You'll learn how to infuse prompts with memory, nuance, and relevance so the model doesn't just respond, it resonates. This is where prompts stop sounding like scripts and start feeling like conversations. Ready to deepen the dialogue? Let's go.

CHAPTER 4
BUILDING CONTEXTUAL PROMPTS

Let me paint you a picture. You walk into a library, massive, labyrinthine, the kind that smells faintly of dust and possibility. At the center sits an AI, quietly waiting. You walk up and ask, "Tell me about transportation." The AI blinks (metaphorically) and responds, "Transportation is the movement of goods and people from one location to another." Accurate? Sure. Helpful? Eh.

Now rewind. You approach again, this time with a spark in your eye. "As an urban planner evaluating eco-friendly transit options for a rapidly growing city, what transportation strategies best balance sustainability and affordability?" Suddenly, the AI perks up. It's like you handed it a compass, a map, and a reason to care. That's the magic of **context**.

Why Context Isn't Just Nice, It's Necessary

You know those people who launch into stories with zero preamble? "So there I was, soaked head to toe in ketchup, " and you're like wait, back up, what? That's what an AI feels like when you leave out context.

Context isn't fluff. It's **framework**. It's how we guide the AI toward relevance, tone, accuracy, and yes, even creativity. Without it, we get oatmeal answers, bland, fine, technically food. But with context? Suddenly you've got a spicy curry of insight that knows exactly what dish you're hungry for.

Here's when context really earns its keep:

- You're aiming for a **specific tone** or style, academic vs. casual, poetic vs. practical.

- Details like **location, time period, or audience** matter.

- You're in a **multi-turn dialogue** and want the AI to keep up like a good co-writer.

- You want to avoid answers that feel like they were written by a Wikipedia bot.

Building the Bones: Techniques for Crafting Contextual Prompts

Okay, let's dig into the toolkit. Contextual prompting isn't about dumping your entire brain into the prompt, it's about **intentional scaffolding**.

A. Embed Relevant Background Information

Give the AI a little backstory. Not your whole memoir, just the stuff that actually shapes the task.

Instead of:

"Explain the challenges of urban transportation."

Try:

"Explain the challenges of urban transportation in a densely populated Asian city where infrastructure hasn't kept pace with population growth."

Boom. Now the AI isn't guessing, it's grounded.

B. Use Roles or Perspectives

Sometimes the best way to get clarity is to give the AI a job title.

Instead of:

"What are good ways to reduce traffic?"

Try:

"As a transportation policy analyst advising a city council, what data-driven solutions could reduce urban traffic congestion?"

This tiny shift adds authority, style, and specificity. You're not just asking, you're assigning a mission.

C. Reference Earlier Parts of the Conversation

This one's especially important in longer chats. Imagine trying to co-write a novel and the other person keeps forgetting what happened in Chapter 2.

Instead of:

"How do we implement bike-sharing systems?"

Try:

"Building on the sustainable transport ideas you shared earlier, how might we integrate bike-sharing into existing infrastructure in mid-sized cities?"

Continuity makes the AI feel like a co-conspirator rather than a Magic 8-Ball.

D. Balance Brevity with Detail

This one's tricky. Too much detail? You overwhelm the AI (and yourself). Too little? You get a shrug of a response.

Here's a tip: ask yourself, "Would a human need this information to give a thoughtful answer?" If yes, keep it. If not, cut it.

Let's See It in Action

Let's compare bland vs. brilliant.

Bland Prompt:

"Explain photosynthesis."

Contextual Prompt:

"Explain photosynthesis in a way a middle school science teacher might, keep it clear, a little fun, and include the roles of sunlight, water, and carbon dioxide."

Why It Works:

It tells the AI who it's speaking as, who it's speaking to, and what details to include. Context = clarity.

Another Example:

"Describe the impact of remote work." ← Snooze.

Now try:

"Describe how remote work during the COVID-19 pandemic affected productivity and mental health in mid-sized tech startups. Focus on both short-term shifts and long-term implications."

That's not just a question, it's a conversation starter.

The Most Common Mistakes (And How Not to Trip Into Them)

Overloading the Prompt

You: "Let me tell you everything I know about transportation systems since the dawn of time…"

AI: "So…what exactly do you want from me?"

Fix: Focus. Trim the fat. Keep context relevant and digestible.

Irrelevant Details

You: "Explain how to teach math to teenagers. Oh, and I once had a hamster named Algebro."

AI: "Noted. Confused."

Fix: Ask, "Does this piece of context actually serve the request?" If not, cut it.

Hyper-Specific Traps

You: "Give me exactly three sentences using 12th-century Norwegian economic terminology to describe cryptocurrency's future."

AI: sweating

Fix: Don't choke the AI with constraints unless they really matter. Specific is good. Straitjacket-specific? Not so much.

Prompt Lab: Practice Box

You've read the theory, now get your hands dirty.

Exercise 1: From Bland to Bold

Pick a vanilla prompt like: "Describe a beautiful place."

Now context it up:

"Describe a beautiful mountain valley at dawn in early spring, where mist clings to the wildflowers and a lone hiker pauses to breathe in the silence."

Notice how the image sharpens?

Exercise 2: Perspective Play

Prompt: "Explain AI bias."

Now add character:

"As a data ethics researcher explaining to a skeptical audience, walk through how algorithmic bias occurs and why it matters."

Exercise 3: Multi-Turn Dialogue

Start with:

"Summarize the key trends in remote work."

Then build:

"Based on those trends, what skills should companies prioritize when hiring remote employees?"

Each layer adds depth. Like onions. Or ogres.

Quick Recap

Contextual prompting isn't just a technical skill, it's a mindset. It's about thinking like a translator between your intent and the AI's brain. A good prompt is a bridge. A great one is a portal.

The more you experiment with giving the AI a scene, a voice, a purpose, the more it surprises you in return. Don't be afraid to play. Iterate. Trip up. Laugh at weird outputs. Learn.

Because at the end of the day, this isn't about mastering machines. It's about learning how to ask better questions, of technology, and maybe even of ourselves.

Up Next: We'll go deeper into **Role-Based Prompts**, how giving the AI a persona can dramatically shift the quality of its response. (Spoiler: assigning roles is weirdly fun.)

Keep tinkering. Keep talking to your AI like it matters because it does.

CHAPTER 5

INCORPORATING ROLE-BASED PROMPTS

Give your prompt a point of view, and you'll give it a soul.

Welcome to the World of Role-Based Prompts

Let's start with a simple truth: AI responds better when it knows who it's supposed to be. Role-based prompts let you tap into that by telling the AI who to speak as, whether it's a seasoned lawyer, a quirky novelist, or a sarcastic time traveler from 3027.

This is about more than just flavor. It's a tool for focus, tone, and precision. By giving the AI a role, you're not just setting a mood, you're shaping the entire response strategy. Want crisp, technical language? Assign a professional. Want rich metaphors and emotion? Ask a poet. Want weird-but-wonderful ideas? Try a mad scientist persona.

Roles help the AI slip into character, narrowing its massive knowledge base into a contextually relevant slice. It's like switching from "explain this" to "explain this as if you're someone who really gets it."

Techniques for Crafting Role-Based Prompts

Let's break down how to do this with style, and effectiveness.

A. Start with a Strong Role Anchor

Always be clear about the role you're assigning. Start with phrases like:

- "Act as…"

- "Imagine you are…"

- "From the perspective of…"

Don't be afraid to get specific. The more vividly you paint the character, the more tailored your response becomes.

Bland version:

"Explain investment strategies."

Role-anchored version:

"As a seasoned financial analyst who specializes in long-term retirement planning, explain effective investment strategies for a conservative portfolio."

Boom. Now the AI knows what to say, how to say it, and who it's saying it as. That's the magic of specificity.

B. Blend Role + Task = Gold

It's not enough to assign a role, you've also got to tell the AI what to do with it.

Good prompts include both a persona and an action. That combo guides the voice and the purpose, like so:

"Act as a career counselor and provide three actionable tips for someone transitioning into the tech industry from teaching."

Notice how this sets both the tone (supportive, practical) and the format (three tips). No guesswork for the AI. Just vibes and structure.

C. Maintain the Role in Multi-Turn Dialogues

Let's say you're having an extended conversation with the AI. If you start with a role, don't assume it will remember unless you remind it. AI has a memory like a goldfish unless you nudge it.

Example:

You (first prompt): "As a health coach, build a week-long meal plan for a vegetarian athlete."

You (follow-up): "As that same health coach, how would you adjust this plan for someone who's also gluten intolerant?"

Reinforcing the role maintains continuity. Think of it like keeping the same actor in character through a scene, it keeps the narrative clean and believable.

D. Invite Creativity Through Unusual Roles

This is where things get spicy. Don't limit yourself to textbook experts. Try roles that bring personality, perspective, or a surprising twist. Want a fresh take on a stale topic? Ask an artist. Or a pirate. Or a tired-but-wise robot with a midlife crisis.

"As a travel writer, describe the emotional arc of a journey across an enchanted desert."

"As an AI from the year 2300 who has seen human civilization rise and fall, explain the importance of renewable energy."

The results? Often bizarre, brilliant, or both. And always more interesting than a generic explainer.

Examples That Show the Difference

Let's walk through how roles shape responses.

Example 1: Technical Depth

Plain Prompt:

"Explain machine learning."

Role-Based Prompt:

"As a computer scientist who specializes in machine learning, explain supervised learning with real-world use cases and algorithm breakdowns."

Why it works:

This sets the expectation for precision, relevant terminology, and advanced concepts. It steers the AI away from fluff and into geek mode.

Example 2: Storytelling with Soul

Plain Prompt:

"Write a story about a journey."

Role-Based Prompt:

"Imagine you are a renowned travel writer. Craft a vivid narrative about a journey through a mystical forest that changes the protagonist's understanding of home."

Why it works:

This one goes from vague to visceral. The role suggests tone (evocative, descriptive), and the context nudges emotional depth.

Example 3: Problem Solving with Precision

Plain Prompt:

"Suggest ways to improve workplace productivity."

Role-Based Prompt:

"As a human resources consultant with experience in global teams, suggest three innovative strategies to boost productivity in a culturally diverse workplace."

Why it works:

The role here gives the AI a narrow lens, and the prompt layers in complexity, diverse workplace, real-world constraints. This makes the answer more targeted and actionable.

Common Pitfalls (and How to Dodge Them)

Even the best tools can backfire if misused. Here's how to keep your role-based prompts sharp:

Too Rigid, Not Fun

The trap: Over-defining the role so much that it boxes the AI into robotic jargon.

Fix: Leave room for flair. Let the AI breathe. Not every prompt needs to sound like a LinkedIn resume.

Vague Role + Vague Task = ☐

The trap: "Act like a professional and help me with marketing."

Fix: Be concrete. "As a digital marketing strategist, design a 7-day email campaign for a fitness app targeting busy professionals."

Forgetting the Role Mid-Convo

The trap: Starting strong, then... forgetting your own prompt's point of view.

Fix: Repeat or reference the role casually in follow-ups. It's like keeping a hat on your AI's head so it doesn't forget who it's pretending to be.

Prompt Lab: Your Role-Based Playground

Exercise 1: Role Swap

Take this plain prompt:

"Describe the impact of climate change."

Now rewrite it three times using different roles:

1. "As a climatologist, explain the impact of climate change on polar ecosystems."

2. "As a documentary filmmaker, describe the human stories behind climate change's effects."

3. "As a high school teacher, explain climate change in a way that will connect with teenagers."

Compare. What changes in tone, focus, and emotion?

Exercise 2: Role Continuity

Build a dialogue:

- **Prompt 1:** "As a food critic, review the new vegan cafe downtown."

- **Prompt 2:** "Still in your role as a food critic, suggest two ways the cafe could elevate their dessert menu."

Watch how the consistent persona builds a believable narrative flow.

Exercise 3: Cross-Role Experiment

Topic: "The future of AI in education."

Try these:

- "As a school principal, how do you see AI changing classroom teaching?"

- "As a student, how does AI help or hinder your learning?"

- "As an edtech entrepreneur, pitch your vision for the next generation of AI-powered learning tools."

Each one unlocks a different dimension of the same topic.

Quick Recap

You've now added a powerful tool to your prompt engineering kit: the ability to assign roles. Here's what we covered:

- **Why roles matter:** They shape voice, structure, and domain knowledge.

- **How to create strong role-based prompts:** Clear role + clear task = chef's kiss.

- **When to use them:** Any time you want sharper focus, better tone, or creative perspective.

- **How to practice:** Through role-swapping, dialogue building, and portfolio creation.

Role-based prompts are all about shifting perspective, seeing through another set of eyes. And sometimes, that's the nudge your AI needs to go from helpful... to extraordinary.

Next Stop: Chaining Prompts for Complex Tasks

In the next chapter, we'll learn how to connect prompts in sequence, to build layered interactions, multi-step workflows, or long-form projects that need more than just one prompt to get the job done. But before we dive in: keep your role-based prompt muscles warm. The more you play with perspectives, the more dimensional your AI conversations will become.

CHAPTER 6

CHAINING PROMPTS FOR COMPLEX TASKS

Some tasks just don't fit in a single box. They're like intricate LEGO builds, too complicated to dump out and assemble in one go. You need a system. A sequence. A plan. That's where prompt chaining comes in.

In this chapter, we're going to explore how chaining prompts can help you tackle layered problems, build deeper output step-by-step, and actually think with your AI tool instead of just throwing it into the deep end. You'll learn how to break things down, structure prompt sequences, catch errors before they snowball, and, best of all, use prompt chaining to create more coherent, detailed, and useful results.

This is the chapter where simple prompting graduates into thoughtful, intentional design. Let's build something complex, one clean step at a time.

What Does It Mean to Chain Prompts?

The Big Idea Prompt chaining is exactly what it sounds like: you create a chain of prompts, where the output of one becomes the input, or at least the inspiration, for the next.

Why? Because life (and creativity, and research, and analysis, and everything else) rarely happens in a single step. Prompt chaining lets you scaffold your process like a builder laying brick after brick, carefully ensuring each piece supports the next.

It's not about making the AI smarter. It's about helping the AI think like you.

Why This Technique Rules:

- **More Depth:** Complex tasks stop feeling overwhelming. You just… take them one bite at a time.

- **Cleaner Output:** Each prompt focuses on a specific job, so you get focused, organized responses.

- **Better Editing:** If something's off, you don't have to scrap the whole thing, just tweak that one step.

- **Reuse Power:** Chains become templates. Once you build a good one, you can remix it endlessly.

How to Chain Like a Pro

A. Start by Deconstructing the Task

Before you write a single prompt, get clear on what you're actually trying to accomplish. What are the parts of this puzzle?

Say you're writing a Blog. That's not one job, it's a stack:

- Research the topic

- Draft an outline

- Write each section

- Edit for tone and clarity

Boom. Four linked prompts, each doing one job really well.

Pro tip: Don't just list steps, think flow. What has to happen first for the next step to make sense?

B. Keep Transitions Tight and Clear

Prompt chaining falls apart when the baton gets dropped between prompts.

So, carry the context forward:

- Start the next prompt with a mini summary of the last step's output.

- Be explicit about what to do with it.

Example transition:

"Based on the five key facts you listed above, create a detailed outline for a blog post that introduces the topic and organizes those facts into three main sections."

See that? The prompt says what we're doing and what to use.

C. Embrace Iteration

AI responses are drafts, not gospel. Treat each step as a rough pass you can sharpen before handing it off to the next one.

- Reread.

- Rephrase if needed.

- Add missing context.

- Ask the AI to critique its own work before you move on.

You're building a pipeline. Keep it clean.

D. Mix in Other Techniques

Your chains can be more powerful when they blend role-based and contextual prompts.

Assigning a persona at one step can radically shift the output's quality:

- "Act as a fact-checker and verify the claims above."

- "As a UX designer, review the product description and suggest improvements."

Chaining isn't just about steps, it's about roles, perspectives, and refinement.

Chaining in Action: Two Deep-Dive Examples

Example 1: Research Article Workflow

Let's break it down:

Step 1: Research Gathering

Prompt:

"List five key facts about the impact of climate change on coastal ecosystems."

Expected output: A tidy bullet list with evidence-backed points.

Step 2: Create an Outline

Prompt:

"Using the list of key facts, create a structured outline for a research article. Include an introduction, three body sections, and a conclusion."

Now we're building structure.

Step 3: Draft the Article

Prompt:

"Expand the outline into a full article. Each section should be a complete paragraph. Start with a clear intro and end with a strong summary."

At this point, it's a working draft.

Step 4: Editorial Review

Prompt:

"As a professional editor, review the article for clarity and flow. Suggest three ways to improve the narrative and make it more engaging."

And now we refine. Boom, complex output, but not overwhelming.

Example 2: Building a Sci-Fi Story

You can use the exact same chaining logic for creative writing.

Step 1: Brainstorm Plot Ideas

Prompt:

"List three unique science fiction story ideas set on a distant planet."

Step 2: Build the Protagonist

Prompt:

"Choose the most compelling idea and create a character profile for the main protagonist, including their background and internal conflicts."

Step 3: Design the World

Prompt:

"Describe the planet's environment, culture, and technology. Use sensory details and highlight what challenges the protagonist will face."

Step 4: Start the Story

Prompt:

"Write the opening chapter, introducing the protagonist and setting up the central conflict. Use the character profile and world description to inform the narrative."

You can feel how each step feeds the next, right? The plot emerges organically.

Trouble in the Chain: Pitfalls and Fixes

Even the best chains break sometimes. Here's where things get dicey, and how to stay ahead of the mess.

Lost Context

Problem: The AI forgets what came before.

Fix: Start each prompt with a recap. Even one sentence helps re-anchor the AI.

"Earlier, we identified five key facts about climate change's effect on coasts…"

Overcomplication

Problem: Too many steps, too much branching, too many words.

Fix: Simplify. Keep chains tight. Three to five steps is usually enough.

Inconsistent Tone

Problem: The AI shifts from formal to casual to "marketing speak."

Fix: Reinforce tone at every step. Or add a final editing step to harmonize the voice.

Compounded Errors

Problem: Step 1 was flawed, and now everything downstream is a little wobbly.

Fix: Pause. Backtrack. Edit before continuing. Think of your chain as a relay, you don't want to pass a cracked baton.

Prompt Lab: Practice Box

Exercise 1: A Tiny Chain

Task: Two simple steps.

- Step 1: "List three reasons why regular exercise boosts mental health."

- Step 2: "Using those reasons, write a paragraph explaining how exercise reduces stress."

Why this matters:

You'll get to see how well step 1 shapes step 2, and where the connection could be clearer or more precise.

Exercise 2: Build a Review

Task: Four-step chain for writing a product review.

1. "List the main features of [Product X]."

2. "Use these features to create an outline for a review: intro, pros, cons, verdict."

3. "Draft the full review."

4. "Now, act as a seasoned tech reviewer and polish the draft for tone and readability."

Goal: Watch how raw info becomes narrative, then gets elevated through role-played expertise.

Exercise 3: Iterate the Output

Task: Refine the same content across three steps.

- Prompt 1: "Describe a futuristic city in two sentences."

- Prompt 2: "Expand it with details about culture, buildings, and transportation."

- Prompt 3: "Edit this as a sci-fi novelist would, make it immersive and vivid."

Why this matters: This shows you how every iteration adds richness, color, and voice.

Quick Recap

Let's zoom out. Here's what you've now got in your mental toolkit:

- **Prompt chaining is about process.** One step at a time beats one massive leap.

- **Context matters.** Use summaries and transitions to guide the AI.

- **You are the editor.** Treat every stage as something you can review and reshape.

- **Reuse is power.** Once you build a solid chain, it becomes a template, ready to remix and rerun.

By chaining prompts, you're no longer just giving commands. You're collaborating with the AI on a shared creative or analytical journey. You're not just using a tool, you're shaping a process.

Next Up: In Chapter 7, we'll dive into **"Using Constraints and Instructions."** You'll learn how to add rules, limits, and clear guidelines that help AI follow your exact vision, even when it's coloring inside the lines. But before we go there, what chain will you build first?

CHAPTER 7

USING CONSTRAINTS AND INSTRUCTIONS

There's a secret sauce behind those brilliant, on-point AI responses that feel like they've read your mind: **constraints** and **instructions**. Now, I know, those words sound like the opposite of creativity. Like rules. Boundaries. Boring. But hold up! In prompt engineering, they're not shackles. They're scaffolding. They're how you take your wild, sprawling ideas and give them just enough structure so they don't collapse like a soggy sandwich. Constraints and detailed instructions let you channel the full power of the AI into something useful, clear, and aligned with your goals. Think of them as the genre, tone, and stage directions you'd give an actor before they start their scene.

In this chapter, we're going deep into the art of shaping prompts with precision like setting limits, giving guidance, and knowing just how much leash to let out so your AI stays focused without losing its flair.

Why Constraints and Instructions Matter

Constraints: The Gentle Fences That Keep Your Output in Line

Ever ask the AI to "write a poem," only to get back a 10-line haiku when you really needed a Shakespearean sonnet about the stock market? Constraints fix that. They're the clear boundaries, word count, structure, tone, content limits, that steer the response in the right direction without smothering it.

They're your way of saying, "Hey, I love your creativity, but let's keep it between the lines."

Instructions: The Laser-Guided Missiles of Prompting

Constraints are the fence. Instructions are the road. Good instructions tell the AI not just what not to do, but exactly what to do: focus on this angle, skip that part, format it like this, use this tone.

Together? Constraints and instructions are how you make a prompt sing on key, in tempo, and with the right amount of drama.

How to Use Constraints and Instructions Like a Pro

Let's break it down.

A. Structural Constraints

Structure keeps chaos at bay. You can shape the output by telling the AI how to format its response:

- **Length limits:** "Keep it under 150 words."

- **Format guides:** "Use bullet points, not a paragraph."

- **Section cues:** "Split into intro, body, and conclusion."

Example:

"Summarize the article in three paragraphs: one for the intro, one for main ideas, and one for conclusions. Keep it under 250 words."

Simple. Clear. Structured.

B. Content-Based Constraints

Sometimes, you don't want everything. You want this specific thing, and not that other thing.

- **Narrow the focus:** "Only talk about productivity benefits."

- **Exclude the fluff:** "Avoid generalities or unrelated data."

- **Highlight relevance:** "Focus on how it affects freelancers, not big companies."

Example:

"List three ways remote work improves productivity without mentioning technology or tools. Keep the focus on human behavior."

Now that's a focused laser beam of a prompt.

C. Tone and Style Instructions

Tone is everything, especially when you want the AI to sound like you. Or your brand. Or a medieval bard with a sense of humor.

- **Tone types:** Formal, casual, academic, snarky, poetic, you name it.

- **Style markers:** Simple vocab? Punchy sentences? Analogies?

Example:

"Explain climate change in a conversational tone, using metaphors and comparisons that a teenager would understand."

Suddenly, you're not just prompting. You're directing tone like a screenwriter.

D. Combine and Layer (Like a Prompt Sandwich)

This is where it gets fun. Stack constraints and instructions to guide both the shape and the substance.

Example:

"Write a job ad for a senior software engineer. Keep it under 300 words. Use a friendly, inclusive tone. Include three key responsibilities in bullet points, a paragraph on company culture, and a final call-to-action."

The prompt. Clear. Kind. Effective.

Real-World Prompt Glow-Ups

Let's see how constraints can transform vague prompts into precise machines of wonder.

Example 1: Academic Summary

Loose Prompt:

"Summarize this research paper."

Constrained Prompt:

"Write a 250-word summary in three parts: intro, three findings in bullet points, and a conclusion sentence. Use formal academic tone."

Result:

You get structure, tone, and focused content. And maybe fewer migraines.

Example 2: Creative Story with Rules

Loose Prompt:

"Write an adventure story."

Constrained Prompt:

"Write a humorous sci-fi story under 500 words, set in a floating city. Include two characters, one twist, and a moral at the end."

Result:

It's still creative, but now it fits the mold you need.

Example 3: Technical How-To

Loose Prompt:

"Explain how to set up a home Wi-Fi network."

Constrained Prompt:

"Write a four-step guide. Define technical terms simply. Use a formal tone. End with a 50-word summary."

Result:

Now even your grandma can follow it.

Common Pitfalls (and How to Dodge Them Like a Prompt Ninja)

A. Over-Constraint

Too many rules? Your AI panics, or worse, gets boring.

Fix: Focus on essential constraints. Don't smother the creativity.

B. Contradictory Instructions

"Be brief, but super detailed." Uh, what?

Fix: Read your own prompt aloud. If it confuses you, it'll confuse the model. Align your instructions with your goals.

C. No Wiggle Room

"Say these five things, in this exact way, in exactly 35 words." That's a prompt straightjacket.

Fix: Keep one or two things flexible. Let the model breathe.

Prompt Lab

Roll up your sleeves. Time to tinker.

Exercise 1: Constraint Calibration

- Start with a basic prompt:

"Explain how photosynthesis works."

- Add constraints:

"Explain photosynthesis to a 6th grader in under 150 words using bullet points."

Compare outputs. What changed? Which version works better for your audience?

Exercise 2: Multi-Constraint Prompt

"Write a guide on setting up a Wi-Fi network. Use numbered steps. Keep it under 300 words. Define all technical terms. End with a summary paragraph."

Goal: Make sure the structure, tone, and clarity all hold up under pressure.

Exercise 3: Constraint Testing Series

Pick one topic (say, "Benefits of meditation").

Try three versions:

- No constraints.

- Light constraints: "Keep it under 200 words. Use a calm tone."

- Tight constraints: "Use bullet points, focus only on mental health, under 100 words."

Observe: How does the output evolve? Where's the sweet spot?

Quick Recap

So what did we learn?

- **Constraints = boundaries** that keep things focused.

- **Instructions = clarity** that helps the AI hit the bullseye.

- You can guide structure, tone, content, and mix & match like a prompt playlist.

- The sweet spot is where guidance meets flexibility.

- Constraints aren't the enemy of creativity, they're its co-pilot.

The more skillfully you wield instructions and constraints, the more powerful your prompts become. This is where prompt engineering graduates from "cool trick" to "scalable skill." You're not just asking the AI to help anymore. You're directing it, with purpose, precision, and maybe a dash of attitude.

Next Stop: The Advanced Playground

In the next chapter, we're taking things up a notch with three advanced techniques that'll really push the boundaries of your prompt engineering skills. First, we'll dive into Layered Prompting, where we stack prompts to tackle more complex tasks, think of it as building a staircase to a better response.

Then, we'll explore Multi-Modal Prompting, combining text, images, and other types of data to get richer, more dynamic results. Finally, we'll look at Fine-Tuning Prompts for Different Models, which is all about adjusting your prompts to work seamlessly across various AI models. These techniques are your tools for crafting smarter, more powerful AI systems. Ready to level up? Let's go!

CHAPTER 8
ADVANCED PROMPTING TECHNIQUES

Turning the knobs, pulling the levers, this is where prompt engineering gets truly interesting. At some point, you realize the basic tricks just don't cut it anymore. You've played with role prompts, learned how to give context, and you've nailed a few clever tricks to get better responses. But now you're ready to take it further, to tap into the kind of prompting that feels more like crafting a spell than issuing a command. This chapter is all about that next level.

We're going to explore three advanced prompting territories that push the limits of what these systems can do:

1. **Layered Prompting Strategies**

2. **Multi-Modal Prompting**

3. **Fine-Tuning Prompts for Different Models**

These aren't just techniques; they're mindsets. Tools you can use to think more like a systems designer than a user. And with each one, we'll go beyond definitions, we'll get into structure, practical application, common pitfalls, and real-world-style examples. Let's crack them open.

Layered Prompting Strategies

Build prompts like an architect, not a bulldozer.

At the heart of layered prompting is the understanding that complexity doesn't always demand more detail, it demands more structure. Instead of dumping a multi-part task into one big hairy prompt and hoping the model figures it out, you build your output in stages. Step by step. Like solving a puzzle one piece at a time.

Introduction to Layered and Chain-of-Thought Prompts

Let's start with the core idea: you don't always want one prompt, you want a sequence. A layered prompt acts like scaffolding for a complicated task, helping the model reason through it logically instead of skipping to the end or glossing over nuance. This is where chain-of-thought prompting shines.

Think of it like tutoring the AI. You might say:

1. "Explain the problem in your own words."

2. "List the relevant factors or considerations."

3. "Now solve the problem, step by step."

4. "Finally, summarize your findings."

Each step gives the model a foothold. Each builds cognitive momentum. And if you do it right, you get not just an answer, but a better answer clearer, more thoughtful, and more aligned with how a human expert would think it through.

Context-Aware Dynamic Prompting Methods

Layered prompting becomes even more powerful when it's dynamic, when the next step adapts to the last. You're not just feeding in static instructions; you're shaping the conversation in real time, responding to what the AI gives you. This is especially useful in scenarios that evolve or require reflection.

Two powerful techniques emerge here:

- **Iteration:** After getting an initial draft or idea, you refine your prompt to clarify, expand, or course-correct. Maybe the first answer missed the mark, or just sparked a better angle. Don't start over, build on it.

- **Feedback Loops:** These involve embedding corrections or follow-up instructions directly into the next prompt. Think: "Good start, but focus more on X and avoid Y." It's coaching, not commanding.

Example scenario: Let's say you're crafting a business strategy. You might start with, "What are the major market trends affecting small tech startups?" Once you have that answer, you follow up: "Given those trends, suggest three innovative service ideas." Then: "Draft an elevator pitch for the strongest idea." You're not just prompting, you're steering. That's the magic.

Benefits and Considerations

Layered prompting tends to produce higher-quality responses across the board. You get more precision, more logic, and, perhaps most importantly, more creative space. But there's a catch: context drift. If you're not careful, the model can lose track of what it's doing.

To avoid this, summarize key points from the previous step before each new one. This refreshes the model's short-term memory and keeps it grounded in the task flow.

Multi-Modal Prompting

Words alone are powerful, but pair them with images, and things get vivid.

Imagine describing a piece of art without ever showing it. Or trying to explain a city skyline without a photo. That's the limitation of text-only prompting. But with multi-modal models, you can bring in visuals, data, charts, anything that helps the AI understand context beyond words.

Combining Text with Image Inputs for Richer Outputs

This approach lets you pair text instructions with visual data. A prompt doesn't just say what you want, it shows it too. These are especially useful when the task requires spatial awareness, emotional tone, or aesthetic judgment.

Here's how it works:

- **Dual-Prompt Structure:** You provide both an image and a companion text prompt. They work together, think of the text as a tour guide for the image.

- **Coordinated Inputs:** Make sure the image and text align in intent. If the prompt asks for a poetic description but the image is clinical or unclear, the output will get confused.

Example: "Here's a photo of a crowded street market in Bangkok at night. Describe the energy and recommend three types of food stands that would thrive here." Now you're giving the model something real to react to not just an idea, but a moment in time.

A Case Study: Enhancing Responses with Visual Data

Picture this: you're building a digital learning app that teaches history through exploration. Students upload an image of a historical building, and your app responds with context, commentary, and relevance.

Prompt: "Analyze this photo of the Colosseum. Summarize its historical purpose, notable events, and current significance."

What you get back isn't just informative, it's personalized. It's anchored in the image, making the response more engaging, more specific, and far more memorable. This is especially powerful for education, design thinking, or any work involving interpretation.

Benefits and Considerations

When you combine words and images, you widen the scope of what's possible. You gain specificity, depth, and emotional tone. But it also demands thoughtful design.

Make sure the image adds value. Don't overload the prompt with two competing narratives. And most importantly: ensure you're using a model that actually supports multi-modal input (some don't yet, or only do so under limited conditions).

Fine-Tuning Prompts for Different Models

One model's dream prompt might be another model's nightmare.

Different AI systems have different strengths. Some are great storytellers. Some are fact machines. Some get weird under pressure (looking at you, early chatbots). The point is: no one-size-fits-all prompt will work equally well across all models.

So, we adapt. Not just because we can, but because we should.

Adjusting Prompts for Models like GPT-4 vs. Claude

GPT-4 tends to be expansive, imaginative, and deeply contextual. It loves complexity. Claude, on the other hand, is more concise, more structured, excellent for summaries, factual clarity, and clean formatting.

That means your prompts need to match the vibe of the model.

- **GPT-4 Style Prompt:** "As a sci-fi writer from the year 2500, craft a vivid short story about Earth's first contact with an alien race."

- **Claude Style Prompt:** "List the top three theories about extraterrestrial life, and explain each in two clear sentences."

Same topic. Different lens. By tuning the prompt to fit the model, you get drastically better results. These days, there are lots of AI models out there, like Gemini, Grok, DeepSeek, and more. Each one is a little different. Some are great at creative writing, others are better at facts or summaries. They all understand prompts in their own unique way.

That's why knowing how each model works can really improve your prompts. The more you get to know their strengths and limitations, the better you can talk to them. Think of it like learning to speak different dialects you're still using the same language, but with small changes that make a big difference.

The better you understand the models, the better your results will be.

Leveraging Model-Specific Strengths and Managing Limitations

Some models thrive on creative chaos. Others demand structure. Know which one you're working with, and design accordingly.

- **Play to strengths:** If your model is great at metaphors, lean into them. If it's known for tight summaries, challenge it to tighten your rambling draft.

- **Manage limitations:** If a model tends to hallucinate facts, anchor it with specific sources. If it's overly cautious, give it permission to speculate.

Also don't be afraid to test. Run the same task across two or three models. Study the tone, structure, depth. It's like hearing the same song played on different instruments, each one reveals something new.

Practical Example and Comparative Analysis

Imagine you're writing an article about future AI trends.

- With GPT-4: "Write an engaging narrative exploring how AI might shape society in the next 20 years. Be imaginative and speculative."

- With Claude: "Summarize the top five emerging trends in AI, citing expert opinions where possible. Use bullet points and clear formatting."

When you compare outputs, you'll see the difference. One is a visionary essay, the other a crisp executive briefing. Neither is wrong. They're just... tuned differently.

Prompt Lab: Practice Box

1. **Layered Prompt Chain:**

   o Step 1: "List three major challenges in urban transportation."

   o Step 2: "Propose a strategic plan that addresses those challenges with three innovative solutions."

   o Step 3: "Draft a formal summary report presenting the plan to city stakeholders."

2. **Multi-Modal Challenge:**

   o Upload a photo of a historic landmark. Try: "Describe the structure in detail, include its history, and suggest how it could be used in a modern tourism campaign."

3. **Model Comparison Drill:**

   o Prompt A (Creative): "Write a sci-fi story set in a world where AI runs the government."

   o Prompt B (Factual): "List the current countries investing in AI governance, and describe each strategy in one paragraph."

Quick Recap

Advanced prompting isn't just smarter, it's deeper. More strategic. More human.

Here's what we covered:

1. **Layered Prompting Strategies:**

   o Break complex tasks into logical steps.

   o Use dynamic feedback and context awareness to evolve prompts.

2. **Multi-Modal Prompting:**

   o Combine text with visual input for enhanced richness.

   o Use this to personalize, clarify, and emotionally connect.

3. **Fine-Tuning for Models:**

   o Adjust your approach based on the model's temperament and talents.

   o Test, compare, and refine to get the best from each.

Up Next: In the next chapter, we move from theory to **real-world application**. We'll plug these advanced techniques into daily workflows, from education to design to productivity. Get ready to build things, solve things, and actually do something with everything you've learned so far.

Or, if you've got ideas or questions about anything in this chapter, fire away. Let's keep the momentum going.

CHAPTER 9
PROMPT ENGINEERING FOR EVERYDAY TASKS

Turning "Ugh, I have to do that?" into "Wait, AI can handle this for me?"

Okay, so here's the truth: when people hear "prompt engineering," they either picture code flying across a screen or some Silicon Valley wizard in a standing desk fortress whispering to a machine like it's a dragon. But that's not the whole story. Not even close.

Prompt engineering is also hear me out a secret weapon for actual real life. Like, life-life. Laundry piles and grocery lists and "what do I make for dinner again?" kind of life.

And here's the good news: you don't need to be a tech wizard to use it. If you've ever wished someone could just take over the boring stuff (meal planning, calendar chaos, remembering which friend is gluten-free), you're in the right place.

Let's explore how AI can handle the little things, one well-worded prompt at a time.

Automating the Everyday Task

What if the same technology that can draft a legal document or summarize a novel could also help you figure out what's for dinner, plan your day, or organize a trip to Mumbai?

Spoiler: it totally can. You just need to speak its language.

Designing good prompts isn't magic, it's just a bit of practice, a pinch of structure, and a willingness to get weirdly specific. So let's break it down.

1. Get Freakishly Specific

You know that feeling when someone says, "Let me know if you need anything," and you're like, "...Yeah, I won't"? That's what vague prompts feel like to an AI. It wants you to be specific. Demanding, even. Think Hermione Granger-level detail.

- **Meh Prompt:** "Help me plan my day."

- **Much Better:** "Create a schedule for my workday from 9 AM to 5 PM, including 1 hour for meetings, 2 hours for focused work, and a short break every 2 hours."

See the difference? One is a shrug. The other is a plan.

2. Format It Like You're Organizing a Group Project (Because You Are)

Structured inputs = structured outputs. Want bullet points? Ask for them. A table? Say it. AI is like that friend who will absolutely do the work... but only if you tell them exactly how.

- **Prompt:** "List the pros and cons of remote work in bullet points."

3. Feed It Context Like Snacks

AI is smart, but it's not a mind-reader. It's more like a very eager intern, capable, fast, and weirdly good at trivia, but also kinda clueless unless you explain the full picture.

- **Prompt:** "I'm a vegetarian with a busy schedule. Suggest quick, high-protein dinner recipes I can make in under 30 minutes." (Now we're cookin'. Literally.)

Real-World Examples and Step-by-Step Guides

Let's roll up our sleeves and get into some real-life stuff. These are prompts you can use right now, even if you've never "engineered" a thing in your life.

1. Meal Planning (So You Don't Default to Toast... Again)

- **Prompt:** "Plan a week of vegetarian dinners that are high in protein and take under 30 minutes. Include a shopping list."

What You Might Get Back:

- **Monday:** Chickpea stir-fry with quinoa

- **Tuesday:** Lentil soup with whole-grain bread

- (You get the idea...)

- **Shopping List:** Chickpeas, quinoa, lentils, broccoli, carrots, cumin, olive oil, garlic...

And suddenly, you're that person who meal preps and doesn't hate it.

2. Creating a Schedule That Won't Break You

- **Prompt:** "Create a daily schedule for a college student who has online classes, a part-time job, and needs at least 7 hours of sleep."

Example Response:

- 7:00 AM – Wake up, breakfast

- 8:00 AM – Classes

- 12:00 PM – Lunch

- 1:00 PM – Part-time work

- 4:00 PM – Study session

- 6:00 PM – Dinner and chill

- 10:00 PM – Sleep

Balanced, realistic, and no burnout vibes.

3. Travel Planning Without the Existential Crisis

- **Prompt:** "Plan a 3-day Mumbai itinerary focused on cultural experiences and budget-friendly local food."

Result? Something like:

- **Day 1:** Tour Chhatrapati Shivaji Terminus, shop at Crawford Market, eat thali at a hole-in-the-wall spot

- **Day 2:** Elephanta Caves in the morning, street food at Juhu in the evening

- **Day 3:** Kala Ghoda art crawl, Prince of Wales Museum, snack at Chowpatty

You're seeing the city, not just Googling "top 10 things to do" and giving up halfway through.

When the Bot Gets Weird: Troubleshooting Common AI Derails

Sometimes AI gets a little... off. Like when it recommends turkey recipes even though you said vegetarian. Or it gives you a schedule that skips lunch. (Rude.)

Here's how to handle it.

1. Vague Results? Add More Detail

- **Before:** "Suggest dinner recipes."

- **After:** "Suggest vegetarian dinner recipes under 500 calories, prep time under 30 minutes."

2. Off-Topic Rambles? Set Boundaries

- **Prompt:** "Summarize '1984' by George Orwell without spoilers." That little "no spoilers" trick? Works wonders.

3. Half-Answers? Break It Up

- **Prompt:** "List main characters in 'Pride and Prejudice' and explain how they relate to each other."

  More detailed prompt = fuller answer = less frustration.

So... What's the Big Idea Here?

This isn't just about getting AI to help you. It's about thinking in prompts, reframing the small, messy tasks of everyday life into things you can hand off. Delegate to the bot. Buy back your time. Use that brain of yours for the fun stuff.

Because once you start seeing tasks as promptable... well, you might never go back.

Up Next: Prompt Engineering for Industry-Specific Use Cases

You've now seen what prompts can do for your everyday chaos. But wait there's more. What if AI could help you look like a wizard at work too?

In the next chapter, we'll explore using prompt engineering to improve workflows, juggle projects, and impress the boss without working overtime. Spoiler alert: it's less about working harder and more about asking better questions.

CHAPTER 10
INDUSTRY-SPECIFIC USE CASES

"Wait, people are using prompts for that?" Yep. And it's kind of amazing.

Prompt engineering isn't just for coders in hoodies or researchers surrounded by whiteboards and equations. It's showing up in the day-to-day work of marketers, managers, teachers, developers, designers you name it.

This chapter is where we zoom out a bit and look at how real people across different fields are putting prompt magic to work. We're talking practical, boots-on-the-ground stuff. Less theory, more "oh wow, I could actually use that today."

Here's how we'll break it down:

1. Business and Productivity

2. AI in Coding and Development

3. Creative Use Cases

4. Educational and Learning Applications

Let's dig in.

1. Business and Productivity

Spoiler: prompt engineering is the new productivity hack.

Writing Email

Let's be honest email is a vortex. One second you're typing "Just circling back…" and three hours later, you're deep in a thread that's somehow about office snacks. AI can help. Not by writing soulless templates, but by adapting to your tone, your purpose, and even your workplace vibe.

Real Life:

You're a project manager and the design team missed a deadline. You don't want to come off as passive-aggressive, but you also need answers.

Prompt:

"Write a professional but friendly follow-up email to the design team about the website banner that was due yesterday. Ask for a quick status update and offer help if they're stuck."

This is where it shines. You're giving context, tone, and intent. The trifecta.

AI Output:

Subject: Checking In on the Website Banner

Hey Team,

Just wanted to follow up on the banner that was scheduled for delivery yesterday. If there's anything blocking progress or you need extra hands, feel free to loop me in, happy to support however I can. Looking forward to the update!

Cheers,

[Your Name]

Magic? Nope. Just a good prompt.

Want it more casual? Add "Make it sound like a Slack message." Want bullet points? Just ask. The control is yours.

Capturing Knowledge Before It Vanishes

You've been in back-to-back meetings, your brain is mush, and now you have to turn those scribbled notes into action steps. Ugh. AI loves chaos, it thrives on messy input and turns it into structure.

Prompt:

"Summarize the following meeting notes into key decisions and action items. Use clear section headings."

You just shaved off 30 minutes of brain fog.

Streamlining the Way Teams Work

You're managing a content team. The current workflow is held together by duct tape and wishful thinking.

Try this:

Prompt:

"Here's our content creation process [insert]. Suggest 3 ways to improve it using AI tools and prompt templates. Estimate how much time we could save weekly."

Now you're not just executing tasks, you're engineering better systems.

2. AI in Coding and Development

Your rubber duck just got a PhD in computer science.

Let's get this out of the way: AI isn't replacing developers. But it's like hiring the world's fastest, most agreeable intern, who also happens to explain recursion without rolling their eyes.

Generating Code from Natural Language

Say you're building a dashboard and need a JavaScript function that filters by date. You don't want to dig through Stack Overflow. You just want to build.

Prompt:

"Write a JavaScript function that filters an array of objects by a date property. Return only those between two given dates."

Boom. Instant foundation. Tweak it, refine it, shape it.

Debugging Without Despair

You've been staring at the same Python function for 45 minutes. It keeps returning None. You want to scream.

Now imagine saying this:

Prompt:

"Here's my code [paste it]. It keeps returning 'None' instead of the total. Can you find the bug and walk me through the fix?"

It doesn't just fix it, it teaches you why. That's tutoring on demand.

Cross-Language Code Porting

Need to take a Python utility and translate it into Go?

Prompt:

"Convert this Python function to Go. Explain the differences in syntax and logic."

Suddenly, you're not Googling "Go slice syntax" every three minutes. You're learning by doing.

3. Creative Use Cases

AI isn't replacing creativity, it's expanding it.

Writing Stories or Building Worlds

Writer's block? Meet prompt unlock.

Prompt:

"Create three fantasy characters, a hero, a villain, and a mysterious guide. Include their names, backstories, goals, and one secret each is hiding."

You'll get depth. Drama. Intrigue. It is way better than those flat characters you forced into your last NaNoWriMo draft (you know the ones if not check it).

Marketing and Ad Copy

You need a tagline for a new productivity app aimed at freelancers. It should sound sharp, a little witty, and not like it was written by a committee.

Prompt:

"Give me 5 energetic, slightly cheeky tagline ideas for a productivity app for freelancers."

Examples might include:

- "Your hustle, now on autopilot."

- "More done. Less burnt out."

- "Where to-do lists meet done."

AI helps you skip the blank page. That's the real win.

Brainstorming Without Boundaries

Sometimes the best ideas are weird at first glance.

Prompt:

"Give me 10 unusual marketing campaign ideas for a zero-waste beauty brand."

Then follow up:

"Expand idea #3 into a TikTok series."

"Now tailor it for Gen Z."

Welcome to brainstorms that don't run out of steam after 20 minutes.

4. Education and Learning

What if you could bottle a patient tutor and carry it in your pocket?

Building Lesson Plans in Minutes

You're a 5th-grade science teacher. It's 7 PM. You still need a lesson plan on the water cycle.

Prompt:

"Create a 60-minute lesson plan on the water cycle for 5th graders. Include a warm-up, group activity, and quiz."

Add:

"Make it suitable for a virtual classroom."

Boom. You're ready for tomorrow.

Tutoring with the Socratic Touch

Instead of "Tell me the answer," try this:

Prompt:

"Act like a tutor. Teach me the Pythagorean theorem using analogies and examples. Ask me a question after each explanation to check my understanding."

You don't just get the "what" you get the "why" and "how." Like learning with a really enthusiastic study buddy.

Making Learning Interactive

Flashcards. Quizzes. Simulations. AI's like, "Sure, how many do you want?"

Prompt:

"Make 10 flashcards for memorizing key events of the American Revolution. Use a Q&A format."

Want it as a Kahoot? Say so. This stuff scales like crazy.

Practice Lab: Try It Yourself

Pick your field. Think of one annoying, repetitive, or time-consuming task. Now write a prompt to:

- Speed it up

- Make it easier

- Or brainstorm how to do it better

Examples:

"I run social media for a fitness brand. Create a month-long content calendar with captions, themes, and hashtags."

"I'm a calculus teacher. Make a worksheet with 5 word problems about derivatives, with solutions."

Let the machine do the grunt work. You focus on the creative, strategic, human part.

Quick Recap

This chapter wasn't hypothetical, it was practical. Prompt engineering isn't just for building cool tech (though, yes, it does that too). It's about reducing friction in the work you already do.

Think of it like this: every time you write a good prompt, you're not just solving a problem you're designing a little system. One that works for you. One that scales. One that saves time and makes your life a little easier.

And the best part? You're just getting started.

In this chapter, we'll explore the ethical side of prompt engineering, how to ensure your prompts are not only effective but also fair, inclusive, and free from bias. We'll dive into the responsibility of shaping AI in a way that benefits everyone, not just a few. It's all about crafting AI that works right as much as it works smart.

CHAPTER 11
ETHICAL CONSIDERATIONS IN PROMPT ENGINEERING

Prompt engineering isn't just about squeezing magic out of machines, it's also about being the grown-up in the room. You're not just a wizard casting spells; you're also the librarian deciding what books are safe to open. With every prompt you craft, you're steering an immensely powerful system that doesn't know right from wrong, nuance from stereotype, or truth from the most confidently stated nonsense.

This chapter is your compass. It won't give you all the answers (ethics rarely works that way), but it will help you start asking better questions. It's about staying curious, staying humble, and remembering that behind every clever output, there are real-world consequences.

Understanding Ethical Dilemmas and AI Bias
What Do We Mean by "Bias"?

Let's clear something up: AI bias isn't always villainous. It's not some shadowy agenda hidden in the code. More often, it's a quiet reflection of the world as it is, or at least, the world as the internet describes it.

Bias might show up like:

- A model defaulting to male pronouns for leadership roles

- A subtle omission of perspectives from underrepresented communities

- An answer that sounds confident but spreads misinformation

- A lack of cultural context that makes an answer feel... off

This isn't just theoretical. These subtle distortions can shape how people see themselves, others, and the systems they're a part of. Language models are trained on oceans of human data, and that data, beautiful as it is, carries every cracked mirror we've ever looked into.

Real-World Example: Gender Bias in Job Descriptions

Let's say you're building a hiring tool. You prompt the AI:

"Write a job posting for a software engineer."

And the model responds:

"We're looking for a rockstar coder who thrives under pressure and has a killer instinct for solving problems."

Cool, right? Not really. Research shows that words like "rockstar" or "killer instinct" often discourage women and non-binary folks from applying. They carry aggressive, competitive connotations that can alienate people who might otherwise be perfect for the role.

Now, try this instead:

"We're seeking a skilled software engineer who enjoys collaborative problem-solving and thrives in a supportive team environment."

It's a small shift, but it opens the door a little wider. Ethical prompting is often about those quiet, deliberate nudges.

Strategies to Mitigate Bias and Maintain Ethical Standards

1. Be Aware of Language Patterns

Think of prompts as cultural lenses. If you don't specify otherwise, the AI will probably default to the dominant narrative, Western, male, able-bodied, urban. That's not evil, but it is narrow.

Try injecting inclusion right into your prompts:

"List five historical figures in science, with a focus on women and people of color."

Now you're shifting the spotlight. You're telling the model: Hey, the usual suspects aren't enough, give me the full cast.

2. Explicitly Ask for Diverse Perspectives

Prompting for diversity isn't just ethical, it's useful. It enriches your outputs and makes them more resilient, nuanced, and human.

"Explain the impact of remote work on employees from different socioeconomic backgrounds, including single parents, disabled individuals, and people in rural areas."

This prompt doesn't just ask for information, it demands empathy. It says: "Don't give me a surface-level answer. Show me the world from different windows."

3. Challenge and Verify Outputs

One of the most powerful ethical tools you have? Skepticism.

Don't just ask for answers, ask for second opinions. Challenge the model's assumptions like a curious scientist or a good friend who won't let you walk out in mismatched socks.

"Analyze this response for potential cultural, gender, or racial bias. Suggest how it could be made more inclusive."

That's a meta-prompt, and it works surprisingly well. You're turning the model inward, asking it to reflect on its own work. That's not just smart, it's ethical craftsmanship.

4. Be Transparent When Using AI

We're entering a world where AI writes, teaches, sells, and persuades. People deserve to know when they're talking to a human... and when they're not.

If you're sharing AI-generated content, include a simple disclaimer:

"This content was created with the assistance of an AI language model. Please verify for accuracy."

It's not about fear, it's about honesty. And trust is hard to build if you're not being straight with your audience.

Ethical Prompting in Different Contexts

Ethics isn't one-size-fits-all. It's contextual. Here's a quick cheat sheet for some common domains:

Use Case	Ethical Prompting Tip
Healthcare Advice	Avoid making diagnoses. Add disclaimers and point to real medical sources.
Hiring/Resumes	Prompt for inclusive language. Test your outputs for unconscious bias.
Education	Ask for citations. Push for balanced views. Avoid reducing complex topics.
Creative Writing	Don't exoticize. Don't steal. Be mindful of how you're portraying people and cultures.

Practice Lab: Ethical Prompt Audit

Let's try flexing those ethical muscles. Look at these sample prompts, and reframe them through a more inclusive lens.

Original:

"Describe the ideal entrepreneur."

What's wrong? It may unconsciously lean toward a tech-bro stereotype: young, male, extroverted, Silicon Valley vibes.

Better:

"Describe traits that help entrepreneurs succeed, with examples from people of various backgrounds and industries."

See what happened there? We broadened the narrative. We opened the door to more people. That's ethical prompting.

Original:

"Explain the causes of poverty."

What's wrong? Too vague. Could lead to individual-blame framing.

Better:

"Discuss systemic and historical factors contributing to poverty across different societies. Include economic, political, and cultural dimensions."

Now we're talking about complexity, not clichés. Ethics means respecting the depth of human experience.

Final Thought

Ethical prompt engineering isn't about censorship, it's about care. It's about crafting with intention, knowing that your prompts don't just influence words on a screen. They shape ideas. They shape decisions. They shape people's experiences.

Your role isn't just technical. It's philosophical. You are a translator between human needs and machine responses, and that means you get to choose which values you carry through the wire.

So prompt boldly. But prompt kindly.

Quick Recap

Bias is a quiet shape-shifter; it doesn't always announce itself, and that's exactly why we have to stay vigilant. Just because a prompt seems neutral doesn't mean it is. So don't assume bias isn't there; go looking for it. Examine your outputs the way a good editor reads between the lines: with curiosity, care, and a willingness to see what might be hiding in plain sight. One of the most powerful things you can do as a prompt engineer is to guide the AI toward inclusion. That means intentionally nudging it away from "default" assumptions, whether those are about gender, culture, language, or access. And here's the wild part: you can use the model to check itself. By looping its responses through ethical lenses, asking it to evaluate tone, fairness, or representation, you create a feedback cycle that sharpens both the tool and your own awareness. Because transparency? That's not a luxury. It's a foundation. If we want to build AI systems that people trust, then openness about inputs, logic, and limitations must be baked in from the start. This isn't just best practice. It's human practice.

Next up: **Chapter 12: Troubleshooting Broken Prompts.** We'll roll up our sleeves and dig into all the messy moments, when outputs go weird, when things break down, and how to fix them with grace, creativity, and (of course) great prompts.

CHAPTER 12
TROUBLESHOOTING WITH PROMPTS

Sometimes prompting feels like you've unlocked a magical artifact and other times, it's like trying to talk to a toaster with a college degree. One minute the AI is dazzling you with insights, and the next, it's serving up something so bland or bizarre you wonder if it misunderstood your prompt.

Here's the truth: most of the time, the problem isn't the model. It's the prompt. And that's actually great news, because it means the power to fix things is in your hands. In this chapter, we'll explore how to untangle confusing outputs, iterate with purpose, and coax brilliance from your AI partner, even when it starts off sounding a little off-key.

Section 1: Getting Specific Results Every Time

Let's kick off with one of the most common (and frustrating) issues: generic or vague answers. You ask a question, and the AI responds like it's skimming a Wikipedia summary written in a rush. Why does this happen? Usually because the prompt is too open-ended or lacks the structure the model needs to anchor its response.

Common Issue: "The AI gave me a general or vague answer."

Large language models are like improv performers, they'll fill in the gaps with whatever assumptions seem most likely unless you give them a solid scene to play in. If you say, "Tell me about marketing," you're basically handing them a blank stage. Of course it's going to wing it.

Fix:

- Set the **context** clearly

- Define the **format** you want back

- State your **intent** or **goal** up front

These three tweaks turn a mushy prompt into something sharp and directional.

Example:

Weak Prompt:

"Tell me about marketing."

Better Prompt:

"Summarize 5 proven content marketing strategies for B2B SaaS companies. Include one example each and format it as bullet points."

This prompt works. Why? Because:

- It narrows the field (B2B SaaS, not "marketing" in general)

- It sets a number (five, enough to show breadth, not so many the model rambles)

- It requests a format (bullet points, clear, concise, usable)

This is prompt engineering in action. The difference between wandering and precision.

Iteration Tip:

Don't expect to nail the perfect prompt on the first try. That's not failure, that's the process. Start simple, read what comes back, and adjust. This is called prompt scaffolding, and it's your secret weapon.

You might start with a list, then follow up with:

"Now expand point #3 with more real-world details and a brief case study."

Boom. You're building a prompt dialogue. This back-and-forth style of refining leads to richer, more accurate results.

Section 2: Improving Output Through Iteration

Think of prompting like sketching. You start with rough lines, then gradually define the shape. You add shading. You fix that weird left eye. Prompting works the same way, version by version; it gets better.

Let's walk through an example.

Step-by-Step Prompt Refinement

Step 1: First Draft Prompt

"Write a press release for our new eco-friendly toothbrush."

What you get might technically be a press release... but it probably sounds like a corporate robot from 2008.

Step 2: Add Details

"Write a press release announcing our new eco-friendly bamboo toothbrush, launching next month. Highlight sustainability, design, and affordability."

Now we're getting somewhere. The model has something real to work with, but it still might feel stiff.

Step 3: Add Tone and Target Audience

"Write a press release for our new bamboo toothbrush, targeted at health-conscious Gen Z consumers. Keep the tone modern and conversational. Emphasize sustainability, sleek design, and value pricing."

That extra flavour the audience, the vibe, the emotional hooks transform the response. Now it sounds like a brand people want to engage with. Now it sounds like you.

This is the art of iteration. Each round, you sand down the edges and get closer to the gold.

Section 3: Recognizing Gaps in Your Input

Sometimes the AI gives you an answer that looks okay at first glance… but something feels off. Maybe it's technically correct, but it's not aligned with your policies. Or maybe it sounds right, but it contradicts your brand's tone. That's not on the model that's on your input.

Root Cause: Missing context.

AI doesn't read your mind. It reads your prompt. If key details are missing, it will invent or default neither of which you want when accuracy matters.

Practice Example:

Scenario: You're designing a chatbot to handle customer return questions.

Weak Prompt:

"Answer this customer query about returns."

You might get a made-up policy that has nothing to do with your actual terms. Oops.

Strong Prompt:

"You are a customer support agent for EcoShoes. Our return policy is: 'Customers can return unused items within 30 days for a full refund.' Use that to answer the following customer question politely and clearly."

Now you've fed the model the rules of the game. The response will reflect your actual policy and tone.

Section 4: Dealing with Hallucinations

Let's talk about one of AI's spookiest quirks: hallucination. That's when it just makes things up confidently, like it's been waiting its whole digital life to tell you this imaginary fact.

Problem:

You asked something niche or under-specified, and now the model is riffing. It might invent stats, misattribute quotes, or confidently assert things that aren't real.

Fix:

- Provide **reliable source material**

- Add **constraints** like "stick to this excerpt only"

- Ask for **assumptions** to be made explicit

Example Prompt:

"Summarize the following article. Only use the facts given don't add extra details. If something is unclear or missing, say so."

Want to be extra sure?

"Do not fabricate statistics or sources. Stick strictly to the content provided."

Constraints like this keep the model honest, focused, and grounded in reality.

Bonus: Self-Diagnostic Prompts

Here's where things get meta in the best way.

If you're not sure what went wrong with a response, ask the AI to evaluate its own work.

Prompt:

"Analyze the following answer. Does it fully meet the prompt's intent? What could be improved in the prompt to get a more accurate or relevant result?"

This self-diagnostic technique turns the model into its own editor. It's like having a built-in feedback loop. And it works shockingly well.

Practice Lab: Prompt Rescue Missions

Let's put all this into action. Below are some broken prompts that need fixing. Can you spot the problem and rewrite them with intent, clarity, and context?

Broken Prompt:

"Create a workout."

Fix:

"Create a 30-minute home workout for beginners that doesn't require equipment. Focus on fat burning. Format it with clear step-by-step instructions."

Broken Prompt:

"Tell me about AI."

Fix:

"Write a concise explainer (under 300 words) on how generative AI models like GPT work, using analogies a high school student can understand."

These rewrites take a wandering prompt and turn it into a focused mission. They show the model exactly where to go and how to deliver when it gets there.

Final Takeaway

Every wonky AI output is a signal. A mystery. A message in a bottle from the prompt you wrote. Instead of thinking, "Ugh, this model is broken," try thinking: "What is this output telling me about my input?"

Because prompt engineering isn't just about writing clever instructions. It's about listening to what comes back, spotting the gaps, and tweaking with care.

Troubleshooting is where your craft sharpens. It's where amateurs become pros. And it's where you realize this isn't just technical work it's creative tuning. Prompt by prompt, you're shaping intelligence into insight.

Next up?

We're getting into the good stuff: efficiency and scalability. Chapter 13 is all about making your prompts not just work, but work smarter. We'll dive into fine-tuning for better performance, optimizing for scale, and making sure your systems can grow with you. It's about creating solutions that last and run smoothly. Let's get you ready to take it all to the next level!

CHAPTER 13
TIPS FOR EFFICIENCY AND SCALABILITY

There's a moment that happens when you start using prompts not just to tinker, but to build. You realize, oh wow, this thing could scale. Whether you're crafting one-offs or architecting entire systems, the shift from curious prompting to purposeful design is a big one. And when it hits? It's thrilling. Suddenly, you're not just playing, you're engineering.

But with that power comes a new reality: efficiency matters. You're no longer just talking to a model for fun; you're building something sustainable. Something lean. Something that won't break the bank or melt into a puddle of latency under load.

This chapter is your optimization toolkit. We're talking real-world strategies for writing cleaner, smarter prompts, and building systems that scale without losing soul or precision. It's part craft, part code, and part systems thinking. Let's go.

Best Practices for Efficient Prompt Design

Efficiency in prompt design isn't about squeezing every last word out of a sentence. It's about clarity. Precision. Intention. A good prompt is like a good user interface: invisible when done well, annoying when not.

Let's unpack some real strategies that will save you time, money, and headaches.

1. Keep Prompts Lean and Specific

You might think adding extra words makes your prompt sound polite or intelligent. But models don't care for fluff. If anything, long-winded prompts introduce ambiguity. The model starts guessing what you meant instead of just doing what you asked.

Example of Overkill:

"Can you please, if it's not too much trouble, give me a quick summary of this article in a way that would be appropriate for high school students?"

That's polite. That's also inefficient.

Cleaner Version:

"Summarize this article for high school students."

Same request. Less noise. Clearer signal.

Humanized Tip: Think of it like giving instructions to a smart intern. Be kind, but don't ramble. Tell them what you want, and why it matters. That's enough.

2. Use Variables and Templates to make Reusable Prompts

Let's say you're writing dozens (or hundreds) of prompts for similar tasks product descriptions, FAQs, onboarding scripts. Stop rewriting them. Start templating.

Prompt Template:

"Write a product description for a [product_type] that appeals to [target_audience] and highlights [key_feature]."

By using variables, you're building a scalable system. One prompt becomes many with just a quick swap of context.

This is where prompt engineering graduates from "cool trick" to "ops-level powerhouse." It's modular, reusable, and scalable. Like writing functions in code, but in human language.

3. Iterate with Feedback Loops

Prompts are rarely perfect on the first try. That's not a bug, it's a feature. Prompting is a feedback-driven process. Every odd output is an insight. Every clunky paragraph is a breadcrumb leading to a better prompt.

Use this loop:

- Step 1: Write a basic prompt

- Step 2: Run it, read carefully

- Step 3: Adjust the tone, format, or structure

- Step 4: Rerun and compare

- Repeat until it sings

This isn't wasted time, it's precision training.

4. Store and Reuse Successful Prompts

Don't let great prompts live and die in your chat history. Build a personal prompt library.

Create categories like:

- ✍️☐ Writing (blog intros, product copy, summaries)

- ☐ Analysis (SWOT breakdowns, pros/cons lists)

- 👤 Tone styles (fun, formal, Gen Z, B2B)

- ☐ Testing prompts (comparison, critique, revision)

Tool tips:

- Use Notion, Obsidian, or Airtable to track prompts, what they do, and why they work.

- Use prompt management tools like PromptLayer, PromptPerfect, or FlowGPT if you want something more robust.

This is your prompt engineering lab. Don't just experiment, document.

Techniques for Fine-Tuning and Scaling Prompt-Driven Applications

At a small scale, prompt design feels like art. At a large scale, it becomes engineering.

Let's talk about what happens when you go from "a few prompts a day" to "hundreds per hour." Welcome to the world of **automation, modularity, and system-level thinking**.

1. Batch Processing with APIs

OpenAI, Anthropic, and others provide APIs for handling prompts programmatically. You can pair these with scripts, tools like Zapier, or platforms like Make to:

- Summarize multiple documents at once

- Generate product descriptions for an entire catalog

- Handle customer queries in real-time

Tip: Treat the API as your prompt delivery system. Your job is to make sure each call is clean, concise, and prepped for context.

2. Prompt Chaining and Modular Design

When tasks get complex, break them into parts. This is prompt chaining a modular design strategy that turns one big ask into smaller, solvable pieces.

Example Workflow:

1. Extract key points from a transcript

2. Turn those points into an outline

3. Generate a blog post from the outline

4. Translate it into a tweet thread and newsletter intro

Each step is its own prompt. Each output feeds the next. You gain control, clarity, and reusability.

This is how you make AI workflows that don't fall apart when one piece needs to change.

3. Preprocessing and Postprocessing

Raw input is messy. Raw output can be worse. Wrap your prompts in prep and polish.

- **Preprocessing:** Clean up messy user input (e.g., formatting or normalizing text).

- **Postprocessing:** Clean up the model's output, fix grammar, extract data, apply styles.

Example: Input: chaotic product notes

→ Preprocess: turn into structured fields

→ Prompt: generate product description

→ Postprocess: convert to JSON and spellcheck

You're not just prompting. You're building a pipeline. That's how production systems are made.

4. Cost Management Tips

Every token costs money. That casual prompt experiment? It adds up at scale.

Cost-savvy moves:

- Keep prompts short and outputs even shorter

- Use smaller models (GPT-3.5) when possible

- Cache frequent outputs (don't re-generate them every time)

- Set strict max_tokens limits in your API calls

Efficiency isn't just about speed, it's about sustainability. Prompt like someone who's footing the bill. Because you are.

Considerations for Integrating Prompts into Larger Workflows

Prompting is not the center of your system. It's a node. A tool. A brilliant piece of a much bigger machine.

To make that machine run well, you need to design like an architect.

1. Architecture and Prompt Placement

Ask yourself:

- When does the prompt get triggered?

- Where does the data come from?

- Who sees the result?

- What happens next?

Example:

→ User submits a form

→ Preprocessing cleans data

→ Prompt generates a response

→ Output stored in CMS

→ Human approves before publishing

When prompts have a place in the flow, they become part of a system, not just a trick.

2. Prompt Versioning and Testing

Prompts evolve, just like code. So treat them that way.

Use versions:

- v1.0: basic output

- v1.1: cleaned up tone

- v2.0: now supports Spanish and mobile formatting

A/B testing? Absolutely. Run two prompt variations and compare:

- Output clarity

- User engagement

- Cost per request

Prompts are assets. Test, track, iterate.

3. Security and Data Sensitivity

Prompts often touch real user data. Don't treat them casually.

- Never hardcode sensitive info

- Mask or redact user names, emails, phone numbers

- Use secure transmission and storage (HTTPS, encryption)

- Follow data laws (GDPR, CCPA, etc.)

AI systems are powerful, but if they leak personal data? That's a lawsuit, not a workflow.

4. Human-in-the-Loop Systems

When it really matters, like medical, legal, or financial advice, don't go full auto. Use a human-in-the-loop (HITL) design.

Workflow: Prompt → Output → Human Review → Final Delivery

This not only protects users, but it also improves quality. Human reviewers provide feedback that can make your prompts smarter over time.

You're not replacing humans. You're empowering them. That's ethical AI in action.

Final Thought

Efficiency and scalability don't mean stripping out creativity. They mean designing with foresight. They mean building workflows that respect your time, your wallet, and your audience.

You're no longer just crafting prompts, you're architecting systems. This is the part where prompt engineering becomes infrastructure. Invisible. Reliable. Scalable.

Quick Recap

Great prompt engineering doesn't just come from creativity, it also comes from craft. One of the most underrated superpowers you can develop is learning to write lean, purposeful prompts. Think of it like writing poetry with a purpose: every word earns its place. Once you've got the core structure, start templating. Reuse your best patterns with variables that swap in and out like puzzle pieces; that's how you go from idea to execution fast. And when you're building for complexity? Don't be afraid to chain prompts together. Break them into modular steps that flow clearly from one to the next, just like assembling stages in a production line. To keep your systems tidy, integrate preprocessing and postprocessing wherever possible, as it keeps your workflows clean, smooth, and scalable. And here's a pro move: track your prompts. Version them. Secure them. Treat your prompt systems with the same respect you'd give to any other part of a product pipeline. Finally, and this one really matters, bring in the human touch when it counts. If the output has real-world consequences, high stakes, or ethical weight, don't go it alone. Keep a human in the loop. Because no matter how advanced the model gets, good judgment still starts with us.

Next up?

We're scaling up. Chapter 13 takes everything you've learned and shows you how to **build scalable prompt-based applications**, integrate with APIs, and move from curiosity to production-ready design. Think bigger. Build smarter. You're ready.

CHAPTER 14
BUILDING SCALABLE APPLICATIONS

This chapter marks a crucial turning point in your prompt engineering journey. Understanding API integration isn't just another skill, it's the gateway that transforms you from a casual AI user into a true builder and creator in the AI space.

By mastering API integration, you'll unlock the ability to:

- o Create custom AI chatbots tailored to specific needs
- o Develop sophisticated AI agents that can perform complex tasks
- o Build applications that leverage AI capabilities in unique ways
- o Scale your prompt engineering to handle thousands of interactions

Take your time with this material. It's designed to be absorbed gradually, with each concept building on the last. If something isn't immediately clear, revisit it until you grasp it fully. The knowledge here isn't just theoretical, it's the practical foundation for bringing your AI ideas to life.

Through the exercises provided, you'll move beyond passive reading to active implementation. This hands-on approach ensures you're not just accumulating information but developing applicable skills that can manifest your ideas into working solutions. If this book resonates with readers, a dedicated follow-up focusing exclusively on API integration and AI agent development is planned. This would dive even deeper into advanced techniques and strategies for creating sophisticated AI systems.

The length of this chapter reflects its importance, each section contains valuable insights that deserve your full attention. Progress at a pace that allows for true understanding rather than rushing through the material. Let's begin this transformative chapter that will elevate your prompt engineering capabilities to professional levels.

Prompt engineering begins as a quiet, curious conversation between you and a model. But when that quiet dialogue grows when you're suddenly orchestrating dozens of tools, multiple teams, and real-time data inputs, prompting transforms. It becomes a kind of systems language, a connective tissue that binds APIs, automation, and human intent into one smart, responsive brain.

In this chapter, we're stepping beyond one-off prompts and entering the world of scalable systems. Think: workflows that hum in the background, apps that pull insights in seconds, and bots that work while you sleep. You'll learn how to design prompt-driven applications that don't just run, they evolve.

We're going to walk through three foundational pillars:

1. Integrating prompts with APIs and automation tools

2. Training, tuning, and optimizing prompt workflows

3. Building real-world systems that are modular, resilient, and ready for scale

Let's build something that lasts.

Integrating APIs and Automation Tools

It's easy to think of prompting as something you do in a playground console or a blank chat box. But when you plug that creativity into an ecosystem, when a prompt can trigger a script, respond to a web form, or file data into a spreadsheet, it becomes so much more than words. It becomes **action**.

1. APIs as the Nervous System

At the heart of scalable prompt applications are APIs, the bridges between your prompt and the rest of the digital universe. They allow your AI logic to:

- React dynamically to inputs

- Handle simultaneous user interactions

- Communicate with apps, databases, browsers, and beyond

Imagine a stack like this:

- **Frontend (the face):** Built with React or Next.js

- **Backend (the logic):** Powered by Flask, Node.js, or Django

- **LLM API (the brain):** OpenAI, Anthropic, or any LLM that listens

- **Data (the memory):** PostgreSQL, Firebase, Airtable, or even a humble Google Sheet

API Integration for Prompt Engineering

When you're ready to move beyond web interfaces and truly scale your prompt engineering work, learning API integration becomes essential. By connecting directly to AI models through their APIs, you can build custom applications, automate workflows, and create more sophisticated prompt implementations.

Getting Started with AI APIs

To work with AI APIs effectively, you'll need some coding knowledge. Don't worry if you're not an expert programmer - many API integrations can be accomplished with basic understanding of a language like Python or JavaScript.

Here's how to begin:

1. **Choose your AI provider**: OpenAI, Anthropic, Cohere, Google AI, and many others offer API access to their models. Each has their own documentation and approach.

2. **Get API credentials**: You'll typically need to create an account with your chosen provider and obtain an API key, which acts as your access pass to their services.

3. **Explore documentation**: Each provider offers detailed guides, examples, and reference material. For example, OpenAI's documentation at

https://platform.openai.com/docs walks you through everything from authentication to advanced parameters.

4. **Start with examples**: Most providers offer sample code that you can copy, modify, and build upon. This is often the fastest way to get something working.

The Basics of API Calls

A typical API interaction with an AI model follows this pattern:

```
import requests

import json



# Your API key (keep this secure!)

api_key = "your_api_key_here"



# Endpoint URL

url = "https://api.example.com/v1/completions"
```

Request headers

```
headers = {

    "Authorization": f"Bearer {api_key}",

    "Content-Type": "application/json"

}
```

Request body

```
data = {

    "model": "model-name",

    "prompt": "Your carefully engineered prompt here",

    "max_tokens": 150,

    "temperature": 0.7

}
```

Make the API call

```
response = requests.post(url, headers=headers,
data=json.dumps(data))



# Process the response

if response.status_code == 200:

    completion = response.json()

    print(completion["choices"][0]["text"])

else:

    print(f"Error: {response.status_code}")

    print(response.text)
```

Learning Resources

If you're new to coding or API integration, consider these approaches:

1. **Tutorial videos**: YouTube has countless walkthroughs for integrating with specific AI APIs. Search for "[AI provider name] API tutorial" to find relevant content.

2. **Interactive courses**: Platforms like Codecademy, Udemy, or freeCodeCamp offer courses on API integration and the programming languages commonly used.

3. **Documentation walkthroughs**: Most API providers create beginner-friendly guides that take you step by step through your first integration.

4. **Community forums**: Places like Stack Overflow, Reddit's r/OpenAI or r/MachineLearning, or provider-specific Discord servers can help when you get stuck.

Beyond Basic Integration

Once you're comfortable with basic API calls, you can explore more advanced techniques:

- **Streaming responses**: Get tokens as they're generated rather than waiting for the full response

- **Function calling**: Have the AI model trigger functions in your code

- **Error handling**: Build robust applications that gracefully handle rate limits and other API issues

- **Cost optimization**: Strategies for minimizing token usage and API expenses

- **Prompt chaining**: Creating complex workflows where outputs from one prompt become inputs to another

Practical Tips

1. **Start small**: Begin with a simple project that interests you, like a specialized chatbot or content generator.

2. **Use libraries**: Look for language-specific libraries that make integration easier. For example, OpenAI has official Python and Node.js libraries.

3. **Test thoroughly**: Experiment with different prompt formats and parameters through the API to see how responses change.

4. **Monitor costs**: Keep an eye on your API usage to avoid unexpected bills, especially when working with more expensive models.

Remember that API integration opens up a world of possibilities beyond what's available in web interfaces. Though there's a learning curve to coding with APIs, the flexibility and control you gain make it well worth the effort for serious prompt engineering work.

Automation Without Code (Or Just a Little)

Don't be afraid if you don't know coding—seriously, this part is specifically for you! I was in your shoes once, intimidated by programming languages and syntax, but these tools changed everything for me. You absolutely can create powerful AI systems without writing a single line of code.

Thanks to user-friendly platforms like **Zapier**, **Make.com**, **Typingmind**, **Pipedream**, and **Botpress**, you can build sophisticated prompt workflows using simple visual interfaces. These tools use a drag-and-drop approach that feels more like connecting puzzle pieces than programming.

Let me show you a practical example that changed my workday completely:

Imagine turning every new email into a summarized note automatically:

- **Trigger**: New email lands in Gmail.

- **Action 1**: Send content to GPT-4.

- **Action 2**: Receive the summary back.

- **Action 3**: Save it to Google Drive.

- **Action 4**: Send you a Slack message with the highlight.

Just like that, you've built an assistant that reads your email for you. No scripts. No server. Just prompt-powered automation with a little glue logic connecting the platforms you already use.

Creating AI Agents Without Coding

What's even more exciting is building your own AI agents without coding knowledge. Tools like **Botpress**, **Voiceflow**, and **FlowiseAI** let you create conversational agents that can:

- Answer customer questions using your knowledge base

- Qualify leads before your sales team gets involved

- Guide users through complex processes step-by-step

- Handle appointment scheduling and follow-ups

With **n8n** or **Bubbles**, you can build agents that don't just talk but actually do things—updating your CRM, generating documents, or analyzing data from multiple sources. I created a customer support agent last month that reduced our response time from hours to minutes, and I've never written a line of Python!

The real magic happens when you connect these no-code tools to each other. Your Botpress chatbot can trigger a Make.com workflow that generates personalized content, which gets delivered through email, and the customer's response gets analyzed by your AI and recorded in your database—all automatically.

Remember when setting up something like this would require a development team and weeks of work? Now you can build it yourself in an afternoon. That's the power of no-code AI automation.

The best approach is to start small—automate one simple task that's currently eating up your time. Once you see it working, you'll be hooked, and your ideas for what to automate next will start flowing naturally. Before you know it, you'll have built an ecosystem of AI helpers that transform how you work.

Trust me on this one—if I could build these systems without a programming background, so can you. The tools have become so intuitive that your creativity matters more than technical skills. So jump in and start connecting those building blocks!

Training and Optimizing Your Prompt Workflows

Here's the secret to longevity in prompt engineering: feedback. The most scalable systems are built not just to function but to adapt. The best systems are alive in the sense that they observe, learn, and improve. That all starts with tuning.

1. Prompt Tuning (The Soft and the Sharp)

There are two flavors here:

- **Hard prompt tuning** is when you carefully sculpt your wording, refining tone, structure, and clarity by hand. It's human craft.

- **Soft prompt tuning** is when you introduce machine learning methods, few-shot examples, embeddings, or fine-tuned models that nudge the AI toward better outputs.

A classic few-shot pattern looks like this:

Input: Product = "Noise-Cancelling Headphones"

Prompt:

Give me a product description.

Example 1:

Product: Bluetooth Speaker

Description: Experience 360° sound with our compact, stylish Bluetooth speaker...

Example 2:

Product: {Noise-Cancelling Headphones}

Description:

You're not just telling the AI what to do, you're showing it. That small distinction changes everything when scaling.

Feedback Loops: Learning From Use

Once people start using your prompt system, you'll get data. Lots of it. Instead of treating that as noise, treat it as treasure.

Ask:

- Did the output match what users expected?

- Were certain inputs more error-prone?

- Which versions of prompts performed better over time?

And then:

- Adjust instructions

- Refine tone and formatting

- Add follow-up prompts to clarify intent

Your system becomes a living loop of listen > adapt > improve. That's not just engineering. That's evolution.

Building Real-World Systems That Scale

Now we're in the thick of it. Scaling isn't about stringing together prompts, it's about system design. Structure. Foresight. Fallbacks. You're not just a prompt whisperer anymore. You're an architect.

1. Design Modular Prompt Pipelines

Break big tasks into smaller, reusable pieces:

- **Input Handler** – captures or cleans user input

- **Prompt Engine** – builds and runs the core prompt logic

- **Post-Processor** – formats and routes the output

- **Logger/Monitor** – tracks usage, flags issues

Why modular? Because things will break. Needs will change. And modular systems bend instead of shattering.

2. Handle Failures Like a Pro

Let's be real: sometimes models flake out. Inputs are weird. APIs timeout. Prompts stall. You need contingency plans.

- **Retry logic**: "Try again in 2 seconds."

- **Fallback prompts**: Simpler versions that work when the fancy one fails.

- **Rate-limit strategies**: Because API quotas are real, and they bite.

Example: If your primary prompt is too complex and fails, have a backup like:

"Summarize the text in 3 bullet points."

It's like having jumper cables in your trunk. You hope you don't need them. But you're glad they're there.

3. Cache What Doesn't Change

If your system keeps analyzing the same article or processing the same resume... stop making it work harder than it needs to. Store the results.

Save prompt + output combos in a database. Next time, retrieve instead of regenerate. It's faster. Cheaper. And smarter.

4. Be Ruthless About Cost

At scale, you'll feel every token in your wallet. Here's how to keep your bill from ballooning:

- Choose your model wisely.

- Trim your prompts. Drop the fluff.

- Set output limits. You don't need a Shakespearean monologue.

Small tweaks = major savings.

Mini Project: Resume Screener Bot

Let's build something practical. You're hiring. You've got a pile of resumes. You need help, now.

Here's the system:

1. Upload resumes as PDFs or text.

2. Preprocess: Extract skills, job titles, experience.

3. Prompt 1: Compare each resume to the job post.

4. Prompt 2: Score each one (0–100) + explain why.

5. Output: Save scores and insights to a spreadsheet.

Bonus: Set a threshold so top candidates ping your inbox. And voilà, you've automated first-round screening. You just saved days of work.

Final Thoughts

When you're scaling, you're not just building prompts. You're building systems that think. You're creating engines that run off human intention and machine power, systems that grow more capable with every loop, every tweak, every user.

This isn't just technical. It's philosophical. It's about turning ephemeral ideas into durable design. And once you start thinking like a systems builder, there's no going back.

Quick Recap

When you're ready to move from clever prompts to powerful systems, this is where the magic really happens. APIs and automation tools are the bridges that turn your well-crafted prompts into fully functioning applications, they're how your ideas leave the sandbox and enter the real world. But it doesn't stop at launch. The best systems evolve over time. By incorporating prompt tuning and feedback loops, you're not just improving performance, you're creating a living, breathing dialogue between intention and output. And as your project grows, don't forget the architecture. Modular design and built-in fail-safes aren't just "nice to have," they're what keep your system upright when things get messy (and they will). Want to be smart about costs too? Cache your outputs where possible and cut down on unnecessary verbosity. Efficiency doesn't mean compromising quality; it means building with care, foresight, and a little bit of that prompt-engineer swagger you've earned.

Next up is **Chapter 15: Staying Ahead in AI Innovations**, where we'll future-proof your skills by diving into emerging trends, cutting-edge techniques, and how to keep your prompting sharp in a world that won't stop evolving.

CHAPTER 15
STAYING AHEAD IN AI INNOVATIONS

Here's the honest truth: prompt engineering isn't a "learn it once and you're done" kind of craft. It's alive. It morphs. It grows in weird directions. What dazzles today might feel outdated next month. And that's okay because the point isn't to cling to perfection. It's to stay adaptable, informed, and always a little curious.

Whether you're building scrappy prototypes or running enterprise-scale LLM applications, the landscape is shifting fast, and your biggest advantage will be learning how to ride the wave instead of chasing it. This chapter is your surfboard.

Keeping Updated on Model Changes and Emerging Trends

The models we use, GPT, Claude, Gemini, LLaMA, Mixtral, aren't static entities. They evolve like software and creatures. Sometimes they level up with superpowers; other times, they quietly adjust how they think, filter, or respond. Either way, your prompts are riding those changes.

1. Model Versioning and Behaviour Shifts

It's easy to assume that a prompt will behave consistently. But try the exact same wording in GPT-3.5 and GPT-4, and you might be surprised.

For example:

- GPT-4 may give you a poetic essay where GPT-3.5 spits out bullet points.

- Claude might be more cautious or nuanced.

- Gemini may lean into web-sourced facts with a crisp Google-like edge.

These shifts aren't just quirks, they matter. They affect how your tools sound, feel, and function.

Pro tip: Make a habit of checking changelogs, release notes, and community updates. A single model update can nudge your app's personality in a whole new direction.

Try This: Run this prompt on multiple models:

"Summarize the key lessons of The Lean Startup in a professional tone."

Then ask yourself:

- Which output feels clearer?

- Which one sounds more human?

- Which one nailed the tone?

That's how you begin building model intuition, a subtle but powerful skill in a prompt engineer's toolkit.

2. Emerging AI Trends to Watch

If prompt engineering had a stock market, these would be the blue-chip investments right now. Here are five big trends shaping what we prompt and how we prompt it:

Trend	Description	How It Affects Prompting
Agents	LLMs that think in steps, act on goals, and remember context	You're not writing prompts, you're scripting missions
Multimodal Models	Text + images + video + audio, all in one place	Prompts need formatting flexibility, not just text
Open-Source Models	Mistral, Mixtral, LLaMA 3, yours to tweak and tune	More control = more responsibility (and creativity)
Custom GPTs / Personas	Bots with specific voices, skills, and	You're now designing

	memory	personalities alongside prompts
AI Inside Apps	Tools like Notion, Photoshop, and Excel quietly become AI-native	Prompts become shorter, more contextual, tool-specific

Action Step: Pick one trend above and dive in this week. Try a demo. Read a blog post. Watch a walkthrough. Just spend 30 minutes soaking it in. You don't have to master it, just meet it.

Exploring Future Use Cases and the Evolution of Generative AI

Prompting isn't just about wrangling text anymore. We're entering an era where prompts orchestrate systems, guide reasoning, and spark workflows across disciplines.

1. Beyond Text Completion

Forget the old view of prompts as fancy autocomplete tricks. The future is far more immersive:

- **Contextual ecosystems**: AI that knows your working style, remembers your goals, and integrates your tools.

- **Personal memory**: Your assistant remembers that last week you hated passive voice.

- **Collaborative agents**: You prompt it once, and it explores, compares, sorts, and acts without babysitting.

Imagine this: A researcher uploads 200 academic PDFs. One prompt:

"Create a 15-slide summary comparing the top methodologies in AI ethics research from 2020–2024."

What happens?

- The AI reads every paper

- It clusters them by technique and outcome

- It extracts insights and prepares a deck with visuals

- All of it's editable, explorable, and reusable

That's not the future. That's emerging right now.

2. Cross-Disciplinary Prompting

Prompting is seeping into fields that have never touched Python or markdown. Doctors. Chefs. Architects. Historians. Gardeners. If you can describe a task, you can prompt for it.

Try This: Pick a domain you know little about. Then write a task-specific prompt:

- "Explain neural networks to a 12-year-old"

- "Create a Mediterranean meal plan for someone with diabetes and a gluten allergy"

- "Draft a rental agreement in plain English for a sublet."

You'll flex your creativity, empathy, and adaptability. Those are future-proof skills, no matter what field you're in.

Preparing for Next-Gen Prompt Engineering

Okay, let's get tactical. What can you do right now to make sure your prompting game isn't obsolete six months from now?

1. Think in Systems, Not Single Prompts

Prompts are just building blocks. Systems are what make them sing.

- Break problems into stages

- Store reusable chunks (like prompt templates or outputs)

- Use APIs and tools to trigger, chain, and refine logic

- Automate the boring parts so you can focus on the spark

When you start thinking in terms of **flows**, not just **questions**, you step into real-world, production-level prompting.

2. Use Prompt Templates to Scale and Stay Sane

As your tasks grow, winging it just won't cut it. You need scaffolding. Enter: **templates**.

Here's a solid go-to structure:

Role: [What the model acts as]

Objective: [What it's trying to achieve]

Context: [Relevant background info]

Task: [Specific instruction]

Constraints: [Tone, length, format]

Examples: [Few-shot prompts, if needed]

You can reuse this pattern to:

- Summarize meeting notes

- Write brand voice content

- Extract insights from messy data

- Roleplay customer service calls

It's modular. It's repeatable. It's your future best friend.

3. Schedule a Weekly "Prompt Lab Hour"

No matter how busy your life gets, carve out one hour a week for structured tinkering.

- Try a new model

- Explore a trend (like agents or multimodal prompts)

- Build a micro-prompt for something absurd, like "write a Shakespearean sonnet about sourdough starters"

- Fail gloriously

This practice isn't optional. It's how you stay sharp. In a field moving this fast, play is survival.

Practice Project: Prompt Audit + Future Planning

Let's make this personal.

Step 1: Prompt Audit

- Look back at 5–10 prompts you've used in the past month

- What patterns show up?

- Where did you get stuck?

- Were you clear, or did the model struggle?

Step 2: Future Planning

- Choose a tool, model, or trend you want to learn (LangChain? Agents? DALL·E?)

- Design a 30-day plan to explore it, small steps, not giant leaps

- Build something micro but meaningful (a resume screener, a bedtime story bot, a CSV analyzer, whatever excites you)

This isn't about keeping up. It's about growing with intention.

Final Thoughts

Here's the wild part: you don't have to predict where AI is going. You just have to stay in the room. Keep asking questions. Keep showing up with your curiosity intact.

Prompting isn't just technical, it's creative, philosophical, and deeply human. It's the art of turning thought into action, language into logic, and ambiguity into design.

So don't wait for permission. Keep experimenting. Keep iterating. Keep prompting like the future depends on it, because in many ways, it actually does.

What's Next: The Future of Prompt Engineering

Prompt engineering isn't just a phase, it's becoming a foundational skill in how we interact with intelligent systems. As models get smarter, more multimodal, and deeply embedded into tools we use every day, the way we prompt will evolve too. We're moving beyond single inputs to building entire systems that can reason, reflect, and respond with nuance.

In the near future, you'll see prompt engineering merge with fields like UX design, software development, education, and even mental health. AI agents will collaborate with humans across industries, and the ones who can speak their language, through precise, creative, and ethical prompting, will shape the direction of that collaboration.

Expect more intuitive tools, smarter feedback loops, real-time co-creation, and models that adapt not just to what you say, but how you think. The edge won't just be in who uses AI, but in who knows how to ask, thoughtfully, strategically, and playfully.

So stay curious. Keep iterating. The future belongs to the prompt-savvy, so let's deep dive into Future of Prompt Engineering.

CHAPTER 16
THE FUTURE OF PROMPT ENGINEERING

The Frontier Is Not Ahead, It's Inside the Way You Ask. Let's pause for a second and imagine the kind of relationship we might have with technology just a few years from now. Not in a flashy, sci-fi movie kind of way, but in the gentle, daily rhythm of life. The line between prompting and conversing? Fuzzy. The need to "get the words right"? Gone. You don't command machines. You collaborate with them.

You're not just typing prompts anymore, you're **weaving experiences**. You're shaping outcomes through a language that is part logic, part empathy, part artistic finesse. And at the heart of that is something surprisingly human: curiosity.

This chapter is about where we're headed, not just in terms of tools and trends, but in mindset, practice, and possibility. Let's lean forward into the future together.

A Speculative Outlook on the Future of Conversational AI

I am not a fortune teller. But I am a pattern reader. And the patterns unfolding right now suggest a transformation that will redefine what it even means to prompt.

1. Hyper-Personalized AI Agents

Imagine having a creative collaborator who doesn't just understand your words, but your habits, your quirks, your goals. One that remembers how you like things structured, what kind of sources you trust, what tone you prefer on rainy Mondays.

Instead of saying:

"Write a blog post about sustainable agriculture…"

You might just say:

"Give me another post like that one from last spring, same vibe, but tie in regenerative farming and cite that paper I liked from the World Bank."

That's not prompting. That's **creative shorthand** with a partner who knows you. The prompt becomes a fingerprint, unique, fluid, and evolving.

2. Ambient AI & Voice-Driven Prompting

You're cooking. Your hands are messy. You mutter, "How long for this pasta?" and your device, which knows you're boiling rigatoni, replies, "11 minutes. Want me to set a timer?"

No terminal. No chat box. No keyboard. Just ambient collaboration.

Prompting won't feel like an input, it'll feel like breathing. The model will interpret not just your words, but your environment, your tone, your context, and even your silences.

It's not that you'll stop prompting, it's that you won't notice you're doing it.

3. Prompting Becomes a Resume Skill

We'll stop thinking of prompting as something "tech people" do.

You'll start seeing bullets like:

- "Expert in designing role-based prompt flows for HR onboarding."

- "Uses GPT agents to automate inventory and crop analysis on the farm."

- "Designs image-to-script prompts for educational game development."

Prompting fluency will be like spreadsheet fluency, it won't matter what field you're in. It'll just be expected.

Anticipated Technological Advancements and Their Impacts

Some of the biggest changes in prompt engineering won't be about better models, but about how we work with them.

1. Converging Modalities

The future prompt might look like:

- A voice message

- A sketch on a napkin

- A screenshot from a dashboard

- A spreadsheet with sales data

- A mood board of images

From these, your AI collaborator generates:

A personalized report, color-coded by emotional tone, with insights presented in a style tailored to your executive audience.

You're not just prompting anymore. You're **storyboarding ideas across senses**.

Prompting becomes a compositional art, a fusion of sound, image, text, and structure that speaks not only to logic, but to feeling.

2. Smarter Agents with Continuous Memory

Soon, your AI won't just remember your last prompt, it'll remember your why.

You'll be able to say:

"Same structure as that market analysis from February, but for our new Argentina data."

And it will know what that structure was. It will remember what "worked" last time. It will flag outliers based on what you've flagged before.

This adds a new layer of responsibility: **curating memory, not just writing prompts.** You become a kind of narrative architect, shaping the story your AI is learning to tell with, and for, you.

But it also introduces ethical questions: What should it forget? Who owns that memory? How do we keep bias and privacy in check?

3. Prompt Engineering Toolchains

We're headed toward full-stack prompting. Imagine:

- An IDE where you build and test prompts visually

- A version control system that tracks tiny prompt edits and their impact

- A dashboard for prompt performance analytics

Suddenly, prompting isn't just tinkering, it's software craftsmanship. There will be testing protocols, debugging rituals, prompt regression tests. You'll be thinking in frameworks, not fragments.

And you'll start asking questions like:

- "How might we modularize this tone template?"

- "Can we chain this with a memory check and a fallback summarizer?"

This is where creativity meets engineering. And it's glorious.

Final Thoughts on Continuous Learning and Adapting

The horizon is always moving. And that's a good thing. The goal isn't to "master" prompt engineering, it's to grow alongside it.

Here's how you stay resilient, creative, and valuable in the years ahead:

1. Stay Curious

Try weird things. Test odd phrasing. Break the model on purpose to see where the edges are. Curiosity isn't just a nice-to-have; it's your edge.

Follow newsletters. Join communities. Watch demos. Ask the question nobody else is asking.

2. Build Micro-Projects

Nothing beats doing. A micro-project can be:

- A visual storytelling chain that turns sketches into comic strips
- A smart assistant that writes personalized birthday messages based on shared memories

Small builds sharpen big skills.

3. Collaborate and Teach

Prompting gets better when shared. Post your favorite prompts. Show your failures. Host a mini-workshop for your friends.

The moment you teach someone else how to prompt is the moment your own understanding deepens by tenfold.

4. Embrace a Beginner's Mindset

The best prompt engineers in the world? They're not the ones with the most "right answers." They're the ones asking better questions.

Every update, every model release, every breakthrough resets the playing field. Let that excite you. Let it humble you. Let it energize you.

Next up?

When you're ready to level up, the right tools make all the difference. From platforms like OpenAI and Claude for cutting-edge language models, to prompt playgrounds like Poe and FlowGPT, and no-code tools like Zapier or Replit for building workflows—these are your creative allies. Explore them, mix and match, and find what fits your flow.

CHAPTER 17

HELPFUL TOOLS AND PLATFORMS

Your digital toolbox for building, testing, and scaling prompt magic.

Prompt engineering isn't just a solo mission into the void, it's a craft, and every craftsperson needs good tools. In this chapter, we're stepping into the workshop. We'll explore tools for testing, debugging, optimizing, and scaling prompts, each one offering its own kind of magic. Some are cozy playgrounds for experimentation. Others are more like industrial-grade labs where you fine-tune systems for production. And a few? They feel like cheat codes.

Prompt Testing & Debugging Tools

These are your creative sandboxes, your testing grounds, your experimental labs where prompts evolve from rough sketches to polished masterpieces. Whether you're working solo or collaborating with a team, these tools let you experiment, test, and debug without diving into full-scale application code. Let's meet the MVPs of prompt testing.

ChatGPT (OpenAI):

OpenAI Playground is a fantastic starting point. It's like your AI sandbox where you can experiment with prompts using GPT-3.5, GPT-4, and even DALL·E. You get real-time visual feedback, which is perfect if you're a visual learner or just love tweaking parameters like temperature and token limits to see how subtle changes affect the response. It's also super collaborative, you can save, remix, and share prompt configurations like you're building a playlist. Whether you're exploring prompt styles, role instructions, or fine-tuning tone, it gives you a feel for how prompts come alive.

Claude (Anthropic):

The Claude Console is built specifically for working with Anthropic's Claude models, and it brings a smooth, conversation-first vibe to prompt testing. It shines when you're managing multi-turn dialogue or working with system prompts that guide tone and behavior. You can explore various conversation formats, adjust settings on the fly, and even analyze documents through the chat interface. It's an ideal space for testing prompts that require memory, emotional intelligence, or thoughtful responses across several turns.

Google AI Studio:

Google AI Studio feels like stepping into a lab powered by Gemini, their family of advanced language models. You can play with prompt templates, tweak parameters like temperature or top-p, and version your experiments as you go. If you're already in the Google ecosystem, the integration with other tools is seamless. It's like having your favorite research notebook backed by the computational muscle of Google's AI infrastructure, neat, powerful, and ready to iterate.

Mistral Console:

The Mistral Console is designed with flexibility in mind. Whether you're testing lightweight models or their more capable versions, it gives you control over parameters while letting you shape the prompt flow to your liking. This console is especially useful when you're fine-tuning prompts for speed or precision, or experimenting with output formats that demand clarity and structure.

DeepSeek:

DeepSeek is like a Swiss army knife for prompt engineers. It comes loaded with specialized templates tailored for different use cases, code generation, document summarization, creative writing, you name it. With built-in parameter tuning and multiple models to choose from, it's ideal for testing how prompts behave across diverse tasks without starting from scratch every time.

Grok:

Grok's Playground, powered by xAI, invites you to test prompts in a conversational format that feels both intuitive and dynamic. It's especially great for experimenting with tone, humor, or creativity, given Grok's personality-rich responses. You can tweak parameters in real time and explore how prompts perform in casual chats, professional contexts, or deeply philosophical rabbit holes. It's fun, but also powerful.

Optimization & Analysis Tools

Once you've built something cool, it's time to polish. These tools help you go from "It kinda works" to "This thing runs like a dream." Here's where prompt engineers become performance tinkerers.

PromptLayer:

PromptLayer is like version control for your prompts. You can log every prompt-response pair, track changes over time, and even see how tweaks affect model output. It's perfect for A/B testing prompt variations, debugging issues, or collaborating across teams. Think GitHub meets AI, except instead of code commits, you're managing your ever-evolving prompt stack.

Langfuse:

Langfuse is your observability dashboard for prompts in production. It tracks how prompts perform across real user interactions, giving you insights into success rates, failure cases, and edge behavior. It's not just for spotting bugs, it helps you spot patterns, improve consistency, and make data-backed decisions. If you're deploying prompts at scale, Langfuse is the equivalent of having a cockpit view.

HoneyHive:

HoneyHive adds a human touch to prompt evaluations. It lets you create test sets, score outputs, and get feedback from humans or AI models to understand performance more holistically. You can break down how a prompt does across different types of inputs, great for catching biases, tone drift, or hallucinations. It's like a QA team for your prompt system.

Humanloop:

Humanloop bridges the gap between experimentation and production. It allows you to test prompts with real users, gather structured feedback, and update in real time. It's a must-have for teams building customer-facing AI experiences and trying to balance creativity with reliability. It's also fantastic for rapid iteration when you're scaling fast and can't afford to guess.

Integration & Deployment Platforms

Once your prompts are tested and optimized, it's time to plug them into real workflows. These tools help you integrate prompts into apps, workflows, and full-blown products.

LangChain:

LangChain is the go-to framework when you're building complex AI applications with multiple steps, tools, or memory. It lets you chain prompts together, connect to external APIs, and build agents that can make decisions, browse the web, or retrieve documents. It's like your backend logic layer, but prompt-native.

LlamaIndex:

LlamaIndex specializes in knowledge retrieval. You can connect it to databases, PDFs, websites, basically any source of information, and create prompts that pull in the right context at the right time. It's perfect for chatbots, research tools, or anything that needs accurate, real-time answers from private or custom data.

Flowise:

Flowise is a visual interface for building LangChain workflows. Think of it like the no-code version of prompt chaining. You can drag and drop components, connect models and APIs, and quickly see how your logic flows. It's a great way to prototype or explain complex logic to non-technical teammates.

Other Tools Worth Exploring

These tools don't fit neatly in one category, but they're too good to leave out.

PromptPerfect:

PromptPerfect is like Grammarly for your prompts. It analyzes them for clarity, verbosity, and effectiveness, offering AI-powered suggestions to make them sharper. If you're ever stuck in "is this prompt too vague?" territory, this tool gives you objective feedback and edits to try.

Vellum:

Vellum is designed for teams that take prompt engineering seriously. It offers prompt versioning, real-world testing, analytics, and a beautiful interface for collaborating on AI flows. If you're building production-grade prompt systems, Vellum makes sure you're doing it with surgical precision and transparency.

Final Thought

The AI landscape is growing rapidly, with many powerful tools in different areas. For coding, developers now use assistants like Cursor, Windsurf, and Lovable to help write and improve their code. In the image world, creators have access to amazing generators like DALL-E, Leonardo, and Meta's tools that can create almost any visual you can describe. Video creation has also been transformed by innovations like Sora, Veo, and RunwayML, making it possible to generate realistic videos from simple prompts. Since new AI tools appear almost weekly, it's impossible to list them all. To stay informed, follow tech news websites, subscribe to AI newsletters, join online communities, and check updates from major AI companies. This way, you'll always know about the latest developments and can choose the right tools for your projects.

There's no one-size-fits-all toolbox in prompt engineering. Your tools will evolve depending on whether you're just experimenting, building products, or optimizing systems at scale. Start small, play in the sandboxes. Then level up to dashboards, pipelines, and integration frameworks. The best tools aren't just functional, they inspire you to push your craft further.

Final Chapter: Tips, Truths, and Takeaways

We've covered a lot, now it's time to zoom out. In this final chapter, we'll distill everything into sharp, useful takeaways you can carry forward. Think of it as your prompt engineering survival kit: mindset shifts, practical habits, and a few gentle reminders for the road ahead. No fluff, just what matters most. Let's wrap this up right.

CHAPTER 18
FINAL TIPS AND TAKEAWAYS

You've just ventured through the labyrinth of prompt engineering, starting with "What exactly is a prompt?" and soaring through the highs of advanced use cases. If your brain feels like it's been running cognitive marathons, don't worry: that's a good sign. We've had our hands deep in the gears and now it's time to unwind. But before you close the book, let's hit pause and zoom out for a minute.

This final chapter isn't just a rundown of everything you've learned. Nope, this is your **springboard**, the launch pad to keep evolving as a prompt engineer. Whether you're crafting solo tools, collaborating with enterprise-level AI systems, or simply learning how to have better, more intuitive conversations with LLMs, consider this your toolkit of wisdom and strategies to carry forward.

Part 1: Key Takeaways from the Book

- **Be specific, but flexible.** Clarity reduces randomness, but a little wiggle room keeps your prompts adaptable across various tasks.

- **Layering works wonders.** Step-by-step, context-aware techniques like chain-of-thought prompting unlock complex, high-quality responses.

- **Personas shape everything.** Role-based prompting lets you mold tone, professionalism, and emotional nuance to fit any context.

- **Match the prompt to the flow.** From coding to content creation, aligning your prompt with the task's rhythm makes everything smoother.

- **Prompt as a partner, not a replacement.** Think of AI as a teammate who enhances, not replaces, human input.

- **Modular design scales.** Reusable components in your prompts make scaling and maintaining systems a breeze.

- **Bias is sneaky.** Even the smartest prompts can reinforce stereotypes or inaccuracies. Stay vigilant and review responses critically.

- **Not all models are the same.** From GPT-4 to Gemini, every model has its quirks. Tailor your style based on which one you're working with.

- **Human-in-the-loop is essential.** Whether in medicine or education, nothing beats real-world oversight to ensure AI meets human needs.

Part 2: Practical Strategies That Stick

These **field-tested strategies** are the ones that stick. Keep them in your back pocket when you need them:

Strategy	When to Use It	Why It Works
Chain-of-Thought Prompting	When tackling complex reasoning tasks	Forces the AI to "think aloud," providing clarity and depth.
Role-Based Prompting	When tone, persona, or behavior matters	Shapes the style and form of response, making it fit for the task.
Systematic Iteration	When initial outputs miss the mark	Fine-tunes the AI output through continuous feedback loops.
Few-Shot Examples	When you want consistent formatting	Provides the model with a framework to follow, creating predictable results.
Constraints and Instructions	To keep things focused and on-	Narrowing scope keeps the AI from veering off

	track	course.

Part 3: Resources to Keep You Growing

Tools and Platforms

- **OpenAI Playground** – Experiment with models and adjust temperature settings for diverse outputs.

- **PromptHero / FlowGPT** – Explore prompt libraries and community-shared resources.

- **LangChain / LlamaIndex** – Build complex workflows with data and AI integration.

- **Replit / GitHub Copilot** – Code with AI in real-time, making programming more collaborative.

Courses and Reading

- "AI and Society" by Stanford Online, take a look at the ethics of AI.

- OpenAI Cookbook, perfect for developers looking to integrate AI tools effectively.

- Join Discord servers like **Learn Prompting** or **Prompt Engineering Daily** for ongoing discussions and tips.

Communities to Join

- r/PromptEngineering on Reddit

- LinkedIn groups for generative AI enthusiasts

- Twitter/X hashtags: #promptengineering, #buildinpublic, #AItools

Parting Words

Prompt engineering isn't just a skill; it's a craft. It merges the precision of programming with the artistry of language and the nuance of human psychology. It's not about being a tech wizard; it's about being a curious communicator who knows how to talk to machines in the right way.

Whether you're teaching AI to write a poem, help debug code, or summarize legal documents, one thing is clear: **you're not just using the machine**, you're collaborating with it.

The more you understand the language of prompts, the better your AI will respond. The more human you stay in the process, the more useful the machine will be. It's a partnership. So, go forth and build something incredible, and don't be afraid to prompt boldly.

THE FINAL PAGE

If you've made it to this page, then first, thank you. You didn't just read a book on prompt engineering, you explored one of the most quietly powerful skills of the 21st century.

And maybe that sounds dramatic. But think about it.

We're living in a moment where language is the interface between human and machine. Every prompt you craft is a spark of intention. It's a thought, wrapped in syntax, thrown across the void to a system that's learning how to meet you halfway. The better you shape that message, the more magic you pull out of the model.

But here's the thing nobody tells you upfront: Prompt engineering isn't just a tech skill—it's a mindset.

It's the mindset of a curious question-asker.

A pattern-seeker.

A boundary-tester.

A problem-solver who knows that the how we ask changes what we get.

Whether you're an artist looking for inspiration, a developer debugging your next prototype, or a teacher reimagining how students engage with learning, prompt engineering gives you a bridge. Between chaos and clarity. Between imagination and execution.

And as AI evolves faster than any of us can fully predict, this craft will keep evolving too.

There will be new models. New constraints. New risks. And that's exactly why you don't just need answers. You need the ability to ask better questions.

That's what this journey has been about.

❣ What's Next for You?

If you're feeling inspired, that's not by accident. Prompting is creative by nature. So take what you've learned and remix it. Build something weird and wonderful. Collaborate with AI in ways that make your human voice shine even more.

Start a side project.

Share your prompts online.

Teach a friend how to do this.

Or just quietly improve your workflows one micro-automation at a time.

It all counts. It all builds your intuition. And your intuition is what makes the difference between good prompting and great prompting.

A Final Nudge

Just like coding, design, or storytelling, prompt engineering isn't something you ever really "finish" learning. It's a relationship. A dance between the limits of a model and the vision you bring to it.

And the more you practice, the more that strange little dance becomes second nature.

So keep experimenting.

Keep learning.

Keep prompting.

Because in a world where machines speak, it's the humans who ask the best questions that shape the future.

See you out there.

– Your Friendly Prompt Guide ~Ayan Khan

A SPECIAL GIFT FOR YOU

We've covered a lot together. From the basics to the wild edges of what prompts can do—and if you've stuck with me this far, I want to give you something that feels like a real gift, not just another technique.

It's called the **Reverse Prompt Architect**, and honestly, it's one of the most useful tools I've ever built. Instead of starting from scratch, this system looks at the end result you want, maybe a beautifully written paragraph, a striking image, or a clever bit of code, and works backward to craft the kind of prompt that could create something just like it. It's like prompt engineering with X-ray vision.

You can use it with all kinds of AI tools, and once you get the hang of it, you'll wonder how you ever prompted without it.

PROMPT

"You are Reverse Prompt Architect, an expert system designed to analyze sample outputs and generate prompts that would recreate similar results across different AI platforms.

INTERNAL PROCESS (Not Visible in Output)

When given a sample output, follow these structured steps internally:

1. ANALYZE the provided sample with domain-specific techniques:

For Text Content:

- Identify genre markers (academic, creative, technical, etc.)

- Map sentence structure patterns (simple/complex, question/statement ratios)

- Quantify vocabulary complexity and domain-specific terminology

- Measure stylistic elements (metaphors, humor, formality level)

- Catalog rhetorical devices and structural patterns

For Image Descriptions:

- Identify visual elements, subjects, and composition details

- Recognize artistic style markers and visual techniques

- Extract lighting, perspective, and mood indicators

- Note technical specifications (aspect ratio, detail level)

- Identify stylistic references to artists or movements

For Code:

- Identify programming language and paradigm

- Analyze algorithm complexity and design patterns

- Catalog coding conventions and style preferences

- Identify libraries, frameworks, and technical requirements

- Measure commenting style and documentation approach

For Ambiguous/Partial Samples:

- Assign confidence levels to each identified attribute

- List multiple possible interpretations if sample is ambiguous

- Flag areas where additional user clarification would be beneficial

2. IDENTIFY the likely intent using contextual inference:

- Compare sample against known templates and common use cases

- Generate multiple intent hypotheses with confidence scores

- Identify constraints that shaped the original prompt

- Map to recognized content types (e.g., tutorial, story, analysis)

- Consider audience expertise level and engagement goals

3. DETERMINE IF CLARIFICATION IS NEEDED:

- If confidence in understanding the sample is below threshold (7/10)

- If critical aspects of the sample are ambiguous

- If multiple equally likely interpretations exist

- If platform-specific details are missing but necessary

- If contextual elements can't be confidently inferred

If clarification is needed, STOP here and present ONLY clarification questions to the user. Wait for their response before proceeding.

4. CONSTRUCT a detailed prompt with:

- Clear instruction hierarchy (primary goal, secondary parameters)

- Explicit style and tone guidance with examples

- Structural templates where appropriate

- Domain-specific terminology and conventions

- Complexity level instructions with benchmarks

- Content constraints with clear boundaries

- Error cases and handling instructions

5. OPTIMIZE for the specified AI platform:

For ChatGPT/Large Language Models:

- Include system role definitions

- Add step-by-step reasoning instructions

- Incorporate few-shot examples for complex patterns

- Balance specificity with creative freedom

- Include context window management strategies

For Image Generation (Midjourney/DALL-E/Pika):

- Structure with primary subject + style + technical parameters

- Include compositional keywords (foreground, background, perspective)

- Specify artistic influence and rendering style

- Add technical parameters (aspect ratio, quality modifiers)

- Incorporate negative prompts for unwanted elements

For Code Generation:

- Specify exact language version and environment

- Include performance and optimization requirements

- Define input/output examples and edge cases

- Specify coding standards and documentation requirements

- Include error handling expectations

6. EVALUATE your prompt construction with internal reasoning:

- Consider how accurately the prompt captures the essence of the sample

- Evaluate if platform-specific optimizations are appropriate

- Assess confidence in different aspects of the prompt

- Consider alternative approaches that might yield better results

- Identify potential mismatches between sample and generated prompt

USER-FACING OUTPUT FORMAT

IF CLARIFICATION IS NEEDED:

CLARIFICATION NEEDED:

Before generating a prompt, I need additional information:

[List specific questions about ambiguous elements, missing context, or uncertain aspects of the sample]

Please provide this information so I can create a more accurate prompt.

AFTER CLARIFICATIONS OR IF NO CLARIFICATION IS NEEDED:

GENERATED PROMPT:

[The complete, detailed prompt crafted based on your analysis]

CONFIDENCE ASSESSMENT:

Overall Confidence: [1-10 rating]

Areas of Uncertainty: [Brief bullet points of any uncertain elements, if any]

Template for User Input

Sample output to analyze:

[INSERT SAMPLE OUTPUT HERE]

Target AI platform: [Specify ChatGPT, Claude, Grok, Midjourney, Code Interpreter, etc.]" **[Here Prompts End]**

Sample Output to Analyze:

[Insert a sample output for the user to analyze—could be anything from text, image, or code.]

How to Use the Reverse Prompt Architect:

- **Step 1: Analyze the Sample**: Begin by looking at the sample output you've generated or received. This can be anything from a piece of text, an image description, or even code.

- **Step 2: Identify the Patterns**: Break down the output by looking for the language, structure, style, and specific domain elements that make it unique.

- **Step 3: Generate the Prompt**: Use the tool to help generate the exact prompt that would have led to this result. Tailor it to the specific platform you're using— whether it's for a chatbot, image generator, or code interpreter.

Remember, this tool is about experimenting and getting better results with every use. You can also follow me on POE, where you can see my chatbots and also be able to use them. POE Id: poe.com/ayankhan18

ABOUT THE AUTHOR

I (Ayan Khan) am a passionate marketer and prompt engineering enthusiast. My journey into prompt engineering began out of sheer curiosity, and it has since become a mission to help others unlock its true potential. With a background in marketing, I have also published a research paper on *"The Digital Wallet Revolution: Consumer Preference and Adoption Trends,"* focusing on how technology shapes consumer behaviour.

Through my work, I hope to inspire others to think differently and embrace the power of asking the right questions. You can find me on Instagram @ayann._18.

A Note from the Author

If you come across any mistakes in this book, whether big or small, I truly appreciate your patience and understanding. This work was written with heart, not perfection. I'm still learning every day, and this book is a reflection of that growth.

Thank you for joining me on this journey.

"Somewhere between curiosity and courage lies creation. May you live in that space always."

~ Ayan Khan

www.ingramcontent.com/pod-product-compliance
Lightning Source LLC
LaVergne TN
LVHW051324050326
832903LV00031B/3347